IPSWICH
AT
WAR

A Military History

By
John Smith, Neil Wylie,
Robert Malster and David Kindred

Published 2002

at 14 Victoria Road, Felixstowe

First published in the United Kingdom in 2002
by

Neil Wylie
14 Victoria Road
Felixstowe
Suffolk IP11 7PT

ISBN 0 9536546 2 1

Printed in Great Britain by:
The Lavenham Press Limited, Lavenham, Suffolk

Front cover: Boer War Memorial unveiling on the Cornhill in 1906

Back Cover: Top -   Volunteer Training Corps Signallers at Ipswich in 1915
Middle - HMS Grafton passing below the Orwell Bridge
Bottom- Raising the sunken N.F.S. Fire Float from
Ipswich Dock in 1941

INTRODUCTION

Following the success of *Felixstowe at War* it was suggested that a similar book on Ipswich might prove popular. Owing to other commitments Phil Hadwen and Peter White were unable to take part in this project, but Ipswich authors Dave Kindred and Bob Malster have joined the team to produce *Ipswich at War*.

The result is a book that shows up considerable differences between Felixstowe and Ipswich and between the effects of war on the two towns. Felixstowe was very much a front line town, with a fort defending the entrance to Harwich harbour; Ipswich was an industrial town which in the Second World War found itself under attack from the air, but there is not in the pictures we have collected the same feeling of its being in the front line. Nevertheless, Ipswich has a story that begs to be told, of building warships in the 18th century, of being a garrison town during the Napoleonic Wars, of Zeppelin attack during the First World War and of being a naval base as well as a centre of munitions production during the Second.

Thanks to the help of many people it has been possible to gather together photographs showing many aspects of a county town at war: fire watchers on the roof of County Hall, Home Guards drilling in the Dales brickyard, rescue squads searching in the ruins of bombed houses, women workers making shells and building aeroplanes in the town's factories, firemen and policemen and members of the ARP organisation going about their duties, and much more. We would particularly like to thank all those who have contributed to this book by lending photographs and providing the information to go with them.

It is sad to see some of the changes that have occurred in the town since the Second World War little more than half a century ago. So many of the industries that contributed to the war effort in 1939-45 have gone: Ransomes & Rapier has closed down and the company's Waterside Works has been cleared, and Ransomes Sims & Jefferies has been acquired by an American firm and the future of Nacton Works, to which the firm moved in the years following the war, is in doubt.

One fact shines out. Ipswich has not seen the shadow of war in the past 50 years. The photographs in this book demonstrate some of the misery that can come out of war, and one can only express the hope that we shall not have to face war again in the future.

DEDICATION

We dedicate this book to the 595 local heroes who gave their lives in the Second World War whose names are recorded in the Book of Remembrance, but have yet to be added to the Town's Cenotaph, along with all those from the area who have died in wars since 1945. We further dedicate the book to all the men and women from the Ipswich area and those who were based here in all the previous conflicts. We are for ever grateful to all whose own lives have been affected in these times and remember with pride and eternal thanks those who paid the ultimate sacrifice for our future.

ACKNOWLEDGEMENTS

Our thanks to all those who have contributed to the production of this book, with special thanks to our families. Whilst every effort has been made to trace owners of any copyright photographs, may we take this opportunity to apologise if any copyright has been unwittingly infringed or thanks omitted. We wish to express our thanks to the following:

Mike Abbott, Graham Austin, George Athroll, Joy Bere, David Cleveland, David Cook, Sarah Chantler (Textron), Mr and Mrs Crisp, Brian Dyes, Peter Driver, Reg Driver, Mr Ellis, Gladys Frost, Doris Fayers, Ganges Association Museum, Lloyd Fenton, Taff Gillingham, Derek Girling, Charlie Girling, Barbara Gilson, Chris Hoskins, Mr and Mrs Holden, Mr and Mrs Havell, Paul Hider, Dave Hunting, Ipswich Borough Museums and Galleries, Ipswich Transport Museum, David Jones, Jasper Collection, Princes Street Fire Station, Marian Jordan, Gordon Kinsey, Mr Kennell, Mrs Leverett, Len Lanigan, John Langford, Martlesham Heath Aviation Society, Mrs S. Marriott, Mr R.J.Nunn, Betty Poole, Mrs Pratt, Jean Pimm, Daphne Preston, Mrs Ransom, Ransomes Archive,University of Reading, Glenda Ray, Suffolk Records Office, Mr Spall, Suffolk Police Headquarters, Suffolk Fire Headquarters, Mr Scrivener, Rex Sheppard, Textron UK Ltd, Gwynn Thomas, Ray and Kath Twidale, Alan Tile, M. Thangamoney, Ken Taylor, Pat Waters, Roy Withams, Joan Whitson, Elaine Whitmore, June Webb, Paul Welham, Dave Wood.

BIBLIOGRAPHY

Published sources:

Kinsey, Gordon	*Martlesham Heath*	Terence Dalton 1975
	Seaplanes Felixstowe	Terence Dalton 1978
Malster,Robert	*A History of Ipswich*	Phillimore 2000
Various contributors	*The Warble magazine*	The Editors 1945
Stokes, Sir William K.B.E.	*A short record of the East Anglian Munitions Committee in the great War 1914-1918*	Silk & Terry Ltd 1919
Various Contributors	*Battalion Souvenir 11th Suffolk Home Guard*	The Editors 1945
Various Contributors	*Ransomes and The Second World War*	Ransomes, Sims & Jefferies Ltd 1945
Various Contributors	*Petroleum Board Eastern Region Souvenir Brochure 1939-1945*	William Chappell Press London E15 1945

Contents

Photographs

1 The Saxon town of Gipeswic suffered from attack more than once, but this man buried in the Butter Market Saxon cemetery excavated in 1987-88 came in peace, though well armed. Buried with him were his shield, two spears, and a broad heavy seax in a scabbard with elaborate copper-alloy fittings which had been suspended from a belt. He came from territory in the upper part of the Rhine valley, probably to trade at the fair that was held on the outskirts of the 7th-century settlement.

2 The inhabitants of Ipswich undoubtedly included some fierce young men who would have made good leaders in war. This drawing by Jayne Brayne is of a Saxon warrior with his horse, which was buried with him in a cemetery at Lakenheath excavated last year by Suffolk archaeologists.

3 The medieval town defences of Ipswich consisted not of a stone wall but of an earthen bank surrounding the central area, with stone gates at the entrances to the town. It might have been thought a somewhat vulnerable bulwark against attack, but the earthen walls were strengthened during the Civil Wars when the Corporation feared that the King's army might strike into East Anglia; in the autumn of 1643 orders were given that 14 men were to keep ward by day and 32 were to watch by night, particular care being taken that the night watch did not go off duty until the ward was set. The West Gate, an imposing structure at the end of Westgate Street, was demolished in 1782 to allow traffic unimpeded access to the town centre

4 When the bank and ditch were no longer needed for defence purposes houses were built along the top of the bank. This photograph of Tower Ramparts looking towards Electric House and the William Pretty factory, taken in the 1930s, shows houses on the ramparts with steps leading up from street level to the front doors. The bank disappeared when the houses were demolished and the area was levelled to form a car park.

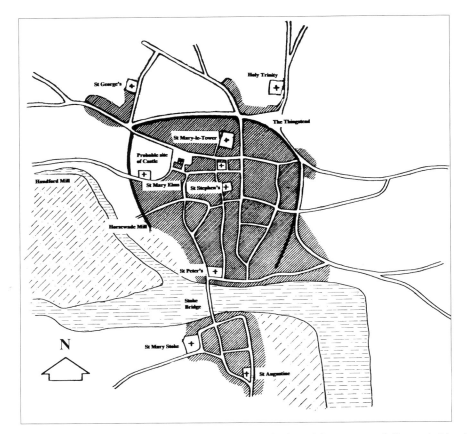

5 The town in early medieval times, showing the probable site of the castle, built in the late 11th century and dismantled by the end of the 12th. The church of St. Mary Elms might have been within the castle precincts, which seem to have been bounded on the north by Westgate Street and on the south by Elm Street. The original bank and ditch seen on this map surrounding the town is thought to have been constructed by the Danes during their occupation of Ipswich, which lasted almost half a century, from 869 to 917.

6 Always a shipbuilding centre, Ipswich produced a galley and its attendant barge for King Edward I in 1294. During the 18th century when the royal dockyards were unable to produce all the vessels needed by the Royal Navy Ipswich shipbuilders, John Barnard among them, received orders to build warships in the town's shipyards. The *Biddeford* is nearing completion on John Barnard's St. Clement's Shipyard in this painting by John Cleveley, reproduced by courtesy of Ipswich Borough Council Museums and Galleries.

7 During the Napoleonic Wars Ipswich was a garrison town and large numbers of troops were based in the vicinity to counter the very real threat of invasion. The maltings on the right of this Victorian photograph of Stoke Bridge was converted into barracks to accommodate some of the regular troops sent to the town. At the same time a hutted camp was built at a cost of about £200,000 on Woodbridge Road to accommodate some 8,000 troops. In 1809 the huts became a hospital used by some of the thousands of soldiers who contracted fever during an ill-fated expedition to the island of Walcheren; more than 200 of the sufferers died in the camp and were buried in Ipswich.

8 A number of tented camps were set up in the coastal area of Suffolk to supplement the barracks at Ipswich and Woodbridge when Britain was perparing for a threatened French invasion in the early 19th century. This is a contemporary picture, dated 1803, of the camp at Bromeswell, from which troops would have been deployed along the coast should an invasion fleet have been sighted. Married quarters were not provided for the soldiers, but there were nonetheless considerable numbers of camp followers, hence the turf-roofed huts in the foreground, which were occupied by these people.

9 The Victorian Militia Depot, built in 1855, stood in Anglesea Road not far from the Barracks. Dating back in origin to Anglo-Saxon times, the Militia was essentially a home-defence force under the control of the Lord Lieutenant of the county, though in 1852 it was placed under the Secretary of State for War. It was absorbed into the Territorial Force in 1908 under the reforms instituted by Lord Haldane, who a little later came to Ipswich to open the new drill hall in Woodbridge Road. The Militia Depot eventually became absorbed into the Anglesea Road hospital.

10 The officers and non-commissioned officers of the 1st Volunteer Battalion, The Suffolk Regiment, at camp at the beginning of the 20th century. There was a long tradition of volunteer soldiering in Ipswich, where the Loyal Ipswich Volunteer Corps was formed for internal defence in 1794 at a period when there were fears of an invasion by the French. It was another invasion scare, in 1859, that led to the formation of the Victorian Volunteer movement and the setting up in Ipswich of the 1st Suffolk Rifle Volunteer Corps, which later also had companies in Woodbridge, Halesworth, Saxmundham and Leiston. In 1908 the Volunteers were absorbed into the new Territorial Force, which in 1921 was renamed the Territorial Army.

11 Volunteer or militia artillerymen outside their Ipswich drill hall in the early years of the 20th century, with the two signallers holding their flags. The two men in khaki are instructors, from the regular army.

12/13 A rifleman of the 1st Suffolk Rifle Volunteer Corps in his green uniform, with his Martini-Henry rifle. While some of the Volunteer units of the Victorian period chose to wear somewhat fanciful uniforms based on those of foreign armies, the Suffolk units had quite plain uniforms, that of the 6th Suffolk Rifle Volunteer Corps in West Suffolk being light grey, with red facings. On the right is Sergt.-Major Sparkes of the 1st Volunteer Battalion, Suffolk Regiment at camp in the early years of the 20th century, wearing the slouch hat that came into use at the time of the Boer War.

14 Taken by William Vick in the second half of the 19th century, this photograph shows men of the Royal Field Artillery grouped around a muzzle-loading field gun at Ipswich Barracks. The gun, and the uniforms, are typical of the Crimean War period, though the picture is of somewhat later date. The Barracks was built by Richard Gooding in 1795 on a site just to the north of where St. Matthew's Street split, one road leading towards London and the other towards Bury St. Edmunds and Norwich. In later years this junction became known as Barrack Corner. The first regiment to move into the barracks was the 2nd or Queen's Regiment of Dragoon Guards, better known as the Queen's Bays since being mounted on bay horses in 1762. The Horse Barracks, as it became known, continued to be used by mounted regiments into the 20th century

15 A gun crew at the Barracks in the late 1880s loading a 9-pounder muzzle-loading gun; the loader is ramming home the charge. At this period two batteries of the Royal Field Artillery were based at the Barracks, each battery having five officers and 130-150 men, and 50-70 horses.

6 Three men of the 73rd Battery Royal Field Artillery in canvas jackets and trousers, the 19th-century equivalent of the later denim fatigues, with a 2-pounder breech-loading field gun and limber photographed by William Vick in 1891.

7 This photograph taken by William Vick on 29 August 1891 is marked on the glass negative "Cpl. Williams' group 73rd Field Battery, Ipswich Barracks". It shows a group of men with two 12-pounder breech-loading field guns outside the gun sheds with their slatted wooden doors. Cpl. Williams is presumably the man sitting between the two guns in the middle of the group.

18 A mounted trumpeter of the Royal Field Artillery rides along Soane Street in 1901 on his way back to the barracks. Such a scene wa commonplace in the days when Ipswich was a garrison town.

19 below left: This early-20th-century postcard is entitled "The long and the short of it". The tall man, a gunner of the Royal Horse Artillery, wears on his right arm the spurs of a rough-rider or riding instructor; the rough-rider was responsible for breaking in new horses. Above it he wears a gunlayer's badge. The shorter man, a driver, wears special protection on his right leg to save it from being crushed between the horse he is riding and the shaft of the limber carrying the ammunition.

20 below right: Artillerymen with a Gatling gun at Ipswich Barracks in the 1890s. The Gatling gun, the world's first machine-gun, was developed during the American Civil War by Richard Jordan Gatling, an inventor of such agricultural implements as a steam plough, and was later manufactured by the Colt Patent Fire Arms Manufacturing Company, of Hartford, Connecticut. The soldiers on this photograph are, standing, left to right, Bombardier Chambers, Corporal Stewart and Bombardier White, and those sitting in front of the gun are Corporal Pike and Sergeant Gale.

21 Officers on the steps of the Officers' Mess at Ipswich Barracks, taken by William Vick in 1891. It is obviously a formal picture, though arranged to appear somewhat informal. At the window on the left two of the mess stewards are looking out as the photographer arranges his subjects, while on the right some women and a child are looking out of another window.

22 In 1892 the men of the 25th and 27th Batteries of the Royal Field Artillery, then based at Ipswich Barracks, were entertained at Holmwood in Woodbridge Road, the home of Mr. James Edward Ransome, one of the directors of the Ipswich engineering firm. William Vick was called in to take some formal photographs of the event, including one of the men sitting down to a meal in the gardens. The picture below shows a group of men of the 25th Battery taken in the garden; a man sitting in the front row is holding a croquet mallet, and another in the left background has broken off from his game of croquet to watch the photographer at work.

23 By the beginning of the 20th century there were few veterans of the Crimean War, 1853-56, left alive. One of the very last was John Gooding, of Ipswich, whose funeral on 6 September 1907 attracted considerable public attention; the hearse, drawn by a pair of black horses, is here being driven up St. Peter's Street past the premises of George Lucas Oxborrow which included the Plough & Sail public house — Oxborrow's Hotel was a later name.

24 Lord Kitchener of Khartoum had strong connections with Suffolk, although he had been born in Ireland. As chief-of-staff and then commander-in-chief in South Africa during the Boer War he became a popular figure and, in Suffolk, something of a local hero, and on his return to this country was made an honorary freeman of Ipswich on 22 September 1902. This postcard by the Ipswich firm of Smiths, Suitall shows the crowd that assembled on Cornhill to welcome him on this occasion. He was later appointed High Steward of the borough.

5 Visits by Lord Kitchener always attracted enormous attention, as may be judged by this view of crowds on the Princes Street bridge waiting to see him on his way from the railway station. The mid-19th-century maltings in the background is now one of Ipswich's most distinctive night clubs.

6 Another view of a crowd on Cornhill gathered to see Lord Kitchener, who is among the group of officers and dignitaries on a platform in the middle of the square, presenting Boer War medals.

27 The unveiling by General Sir John French of the Boer War memorial on Cornhill on 29 September 1906, with the Head Post Office in the background. Designed by sculptor Albert Toft, the memorial depicted a soldier, with his rifle reversed in mourning, standing by the grave of comrade. The memorial was later removed to Christchurch Park, where it stands near the Cenotaph erected after the First World War.

28/29 Another view of the unveiling of the South African War Memorial, which commemorated not only men of the Suffolk Regiment but also the men of East Suffolk serving in other regiments who had fallen in the South African War. On parade were men of the 1st Battalion, The Suffolk Regiment, then stationed at Woolwich, with their band and drums, and members of the 1st Volunteer Battalion Suffolk Regiment under Colonel W.A. Churchman, as well as the Royal Horse Artillery from the Barracks. The picture below, taken from the Town Hall, shows the crowds on the Cornhill and people watching from windows and balconies of business premises surrounding the square; such events then attracted hordes of spectators.

30/31 In the early years of the 20th century military planners took the view that troops equipped with bicycles would be most useful in defending the coast as the cycles gave them a mobility only enjoyed up to then by the cavalry, who tended to be much more conspicuous. Men who were keen on the sport of cycling joined Cyclists battalions of the Volunteer corps. The photograph above shows cyclists on parade at summer camp about 1902; the bicycles are all equipped with special fittings to carry a rifle. The lower picture, taken in 1906 in Burlington Road, is of new recruits to the 6th Cyclists Companyof 1ˢᵗ V. B. Suffolk Regiment with their cycles; further along are existing members of the battalion, in uniform.

32/33 The short reign of King Edward VII was brought to an end by his death in 1910. The day of his funeral, 20 May, was the occasion for memorial services in every church in Ipswich, and the various units of the Territorial Force, together with the Boy Scouts, attended an open-air service on the Portman Road sports ground organised by Colonel W.A. Churchman, commanding officer of what was by then the 4th Battalion, The Suffolk Regiment. These two postcards, part of a series produced by a local photographer, show the troops drawn up in a hollow square; the lower picture includes the Boy Scouts in the foreground.

34 The Secretary of State for War, Lord Haldane, came to Ipswich on 13 May 1911 to open a new drill hall at the bottom of Woodbridge Road, built at a cost of £3,000 for the 1st East Anglian Field Ambulance and the Suffolk companies of the Essex & Suffolk Cyclist Battalion. As he arrived at Ipswich station he was received by a guard of honour of the 4th Battalion The Suffolk Regiment, who in the picture above await Lord Haldane's arrival.

35 Lord Haldane, in top hat, inspects the guard of honour outside the station.

36 Lord Haldane inspecting nurses of a Voluntary Aid Detachment during his visit to Ipswich.

37 A guard of honour of the Essex & Suffolk Cyclist Battalion present arms as Lord Haldane returns to his car after opening the new drill hall, which is now the International Community Centre of the Ipswich Caribbean Association.

38/39 Lord Kitchener, wearing civilian clothes rather than his field marshal's uniform, attended a Boy Scout rally on the Portman Road sports ground on 31 May 1911. More than 600 Scouts, together with members of the Church Lads Brigade, the Boys Brigade and the St. John Ambulance Brigade attended the rally. In the picture above Lord Kitchener can be seen inspecting some of the Scouts, and in the photograph below he is speaking to the boys, who all seem to be listening intently to the great man. In the foreground a cine film of the occasion is being shot for showing next day in one of the local cinemas. An Ipswichian remarked to one of the Scouts who had come up from the country, "Well, my little man, so you've come in to see Lord Kitchener". He was somewhat taken aback to receive the reply "Lord Kitchener is coming to see us".

40/41 Early aircraft were unreliable and accidents were frequent. One of those accidents claimed the life of Captain Eustace Loraine, of Bramford, on 5 July 1912, when his Nieuport aeroplane stalled at 400 feet and crashed into the ground as it took off from Larkhill, on Salisbury Plain. Also killed was Captain Loraine's passenger, Staff Sergeant Wilson, who had been only the second non-commissioned officer in the British Army to qualify as a pilot. Captain Loraine's body was taken by train to Bramford, where a military funeral was held. More than 200 members of his regiment, the Grenadier Guards, took part in the funeral; they are seen in the picture, with arms reversed, marching to St. Mary's Church. Captain Loraine's gravestone at Bramford, under the shadow of the church tower, is now hardly decipherable, but a memorial to the two airmen on Salisbury Plain has been restored by members of the Royal Engineers.

42 Shotley Gate photographed in 1906 shortly after the Royal Navy Training Establishment opened. In the background moored beyond the Admiralty Pier is HMS *Ganges*.

43 Below is HMS *Ganges,* built in India and launched on 10 November 1821 as a second rate of 84 guns, 2284 tons with a crew of 700. Her design was based on a French vessel captured by Admiral Nelson at the battle of the Nile. *Ganges* was the last sailing ship to be a sea-going flagship, and after service in different parts of the world was paid off at Sheerness in 1861. In 1865 she was fitted out as a training ship for boys at Falmouth, and in 1899 was transferred to Harwich. In 1906 she left Shotley under a new name HMS *Tenedos* III to serve elsewhere in Home waters, becoming *Indus V* in 1910 and *Impregnable III* in 1922. She was sold out of service in 1929 and broken up in 1930.

44 HMS *Ganges* II, known as the Twicer, came to Shotley when the original *Ganges* left in 1906. Built as the iron screw ship *Minotaur* by the Thames Iron Works in 1863, she served as part of the Shotley Training Establishment until 1922.

46 The main gate of HMS *Ganges*. The figurehead on the right was taken from the training ship HMS *St Vincent*, which was moored at Portsmouth until 1906 when the boys under training together with three Warrant Officers and three Instructors were moved to HMS *Ganges* at Shotley. This figurehead was replaced by a plaster replica in 1945. The figurehead on the left was that of HMS *Caledonia*, which entered service in 1810 as HMS *Impregnable;* she became a training ship in 1862 and was renamed HMS *Kent* in 1888 and again renamed HMS *Caledonia* in 1891 when she became a boys' training ship moored in the Firth of Forth at Queensferry. She was paid off in 1906 and the boys and staff were transferred to HMS *Ganges* at Shotley.

46/47 Two views of the covered way at the Royal Navy Training Establishment. Above is the entrance, with the capstan and bits in the foreground. The picture below shows some of the boys from the various messes that branched off from the covered way.

48 The Quarter Deck at the Royal Navy Training Establishment, Shotley. In the foreground can be seen the capstan and bits that were transferred, along with the figurehead in the background, to the Establishment in 1905.

49 Under the watchful eye of their instructor boys carry equipment down the Boat Pier, while others work on the boats.

50/51 Above, the Farman biplane flown by Major Gordon, of the Royal Marine Light Infantry, having landed at Shotley attracted the attention of most of the boys. In the background is the mast at the Training Establishment. Below is a Short S.41 seaplane, possibly that flown to Shotley in August 1912 by Charles Samson, being manoeuvred on to the slipway by a team of matelots. A temporary corrugated-iron shed was erected on the Shotley foreshore to accommodate the seaplane while it was operating in the Harwich area.

52 The first mast at the Shore Establishment was erected in 1907 using the foremast of a steam corvette, HMS *Cordelia,* broken up in 1904. Here we see the boys gathered round the mast with others in the rigging.

53 There were camps all around Ipswich during the First World War, the heathland to the east of the town being home to several camps in which units were accommodated either for early training or in preparation for service in France. On 6th November, 1914, the 4th Suffolks entrained at St. Botolph's Station in Colchester singing "Mr. Kaïser, Mr. Kaiser, you're the cause of all the trouble, the cause of all the pain," and a few days later King George V travelled to Colchester and then on to Martlesham Heath to see East Anglian units that were preparing for action. The Young Men's Christian Association was to the fore in providing for the troops, many of whom had never left their homes before. In the picture are the staff of the YMCA marquee at the camp on Bixley Heath.

54/55 Postcards and letters home were supposed to be devoid of information that could be useful to the enemy, including of course the location of military installations. These postcards, however, indicate that the senders were in camps on Foxhall Heath and at Ipswich, though quite where the latter camp was is unknown. The Foxhall Heath camp was apparently a depot for training new recruits, and the other was probably the same.

FOXHALL HEATH.

THERE'S a certain place called Foxhall Heath,
  Near good old Ipswich Town,
And if I could only but escape
  I'd ne'er go back again.

The place is noted far and wide,
  A Depot for Recruits,
Trench Digging and Route Marches
  Which wears out all your boots.

The Scenery is beautiful,
  You should see some of the hills,
Where we go through a performance,
  Which the Poets call " Swedish Drill."

We rise each morn at half-past five,
  Just when Reveille blows,
And practice rapid-marching,
  In charge of N.C.O's.

Sometimes we go shooting,
  To try and earn our Bounties,
But some of the shots I fired myself,
  Could be found in several counties.

Foxhall Heath is all right in its place,
  With its valleys and its dells,
But I would rather be in France,
  Or else the Dardanelles.

To find a place like Foxhall Heath,
  Many miles you'd have to roam,
But I wish the War was over,
  And I was back at home.

IPSWICH CAMP.

THERE'S an isolated, desolated spot I'd like to mention,
  Where all you hear is " Stand at Ease," " Slope Arms,"
    " Quick March." " Attention."
It's miles away from anywhere, by Gad, it's a rum 'un,
A chap lived there for fifty years and never saw a woman.

There are lots of little tents, all dotted here and there.
For those that have to live inside, I've offered many a prayer
Inside the tents there's RATS as big as any nanny goat,
Last night a soldier saw one trying on his overcoat.

It's dust up to your eyebrows, you get it in your ears,
But into it you've got to go, without a sign of fear,
And when you've had a bath of it, you just set to and
    groom.
And get cleaned up for next Parade, or else it's " Orderly
    Room."

Week in, week out, from morn till night, with full pack and
    a rifle,
Like Jack and Jill, you climb the hills, of course that's just
    a trifle.
" Slope Arms," " Fix Bayonets," then " Present," they fairly
    put you through it,
And as you stagger to your tent the Sergeant shouts " Jump
    to it "

With tunic, boots and puttees off, you quickly get the habit
You gallop up and down the camp just like a blooming rabbit
" Heads backward bend," " Arms upward stretch," " Heels
    raise," then " Ranks change places,"
And later on they make you put your kneecaps where your
    face is.

Now when this war is over and we've captured Kaiser Billy
To shoot him would be merciful and absolutely silly,
Just send him down to IPSWICH among the Rats
    and Clay,
And I'll bet he won't be long before he droops and fades away

BUT WE'RE NOT DOWNHEARTED YET.

56/58 In contrast to the tent on Bixley Heath nearby, the YMCA at the camp on Warren Heath, now the site of Sainsbury's superstore and new housing areas, was housed in a large and roomy hut. Perhaps at an earlier stage in the growth of the camp the YMCA at Warren Heath had also been in a tent, because the postcard of YMCA staff and soldiers in the doorway of the hut refers to the YMCA "tent". At any rate it would have been somewhat larger than the bell tents shown below right; the flap of this postcard could be lifted to reveal views of the Ipswich area.

59 During the 1914-18 war many horses were requisitioned from the farms and from other sources for the army. Here army horses are being shod outside 12 St. Margaret's Plain; in the doorway is shoeing smith George Cook.

60 The Suffolk Yeomanry (Duke of York's Own Loyal Suffolk Hussars) has a long and distinguished history, including service in two world wars The yeomanry were originally a volunteer force recruited largely from the farming community, and comprising men who were able to bring their own horses with them when embodied for service. In some cases several generations of the same family served in the regiment. The picture below is of Cheveley Rickett when serving in the 1914-18 war.

1/62 When war broke out in 1914 the Suffolk Regiment had six battalions, the 1st Battalion being in the Sudan and the 2nd Battalion at the Curragh
n Ireland. Three of the battalions were Territorial battalions, and in the course of the war no fewer than 16 other battalions were raised, the Suffolk
eomanry being converted into the 15th Battalion in 1917. While young men swarmed to the recruiting offices to join these battalions those who
vere too old for regular service joined the Suffolk Volunteer Training Corps, like the signallers in the picture below with their flags and signal lamps.
t is thought that the picture above of men forming up in ranks on the Cornhill shows men enlisting in this Volunteer Training Corps, a kind of First
World War Dad's Army.

BEWARE OF SPIES.

DON'T TALK.   THE ENEMY HAS EARS EVERYWHERE.

DON'T imagine that everyone who SPEAKS ENGLISH is to be trusted, and that every UNIFORM covers a FRIEND.

DON'T exchange confidences with CASUAL COMPANIONS or when travelling at home or abroad.

DON'T trust STRANGERS who write to you, who offer gifts or hospitality, or who tell you their secrets.

DON'T carry about with you or show MAPS, PLANS, ORDERS, or any naval or military document.

DON'T hesitate to PREVENT and to REPORT at once any leakage of information or any suspicious action.

DON'T mention naval or military matters in your LETTERS. They have a habit of getting into print to the advantage of the enemy.

DON'T imagine that private DIARIES or NOTE BOOKS will keep secrets.   They sometimes get lost or stolen.

DON'T leave written SCRAPS OF PAPER about.   BURN them. They might tell tales.

DON'T forget that a CHANCE WORD or a SCRAP OF PAPER may help your enemy and SLAY YOUR FRIEND.

W 18061—5748   100,000   3/16   H W V (P 1514)   P. 15/901

Page One. | Permit Book | No | 228024

Issued at _Town Hall, Ipswich_

Date _6. 7. 17_ Also holds Books Nos. [_____

Issued to :—Style or Title _Miss_
SURNAME [in capitals] _SHEPPARD_
Christian Names _Eva_
Postal Address _"North View"_ _Tuddenham Rd Ipswich_

Signature of Holder { _E. Sheppard_

PERSONAL DESCRIPTION.

Height _5_ ft. _6½_ ins.
Sex _Female_
Build _medium_
Hair, colour _dk brown_
Eyes, colour _grey_
Distinctive Marks _nil_

Entered by _J Jennings_

Page Seven. | Book | No | 228024

PERMIT No. X 21832

To all whom it may concern.

By virtue of the powers vested in me under the Defence of the Realm Regulations I hereby _grant_ permission to

M_iss E Sheppard_

of _Tuddenham Rd. Ips_

to **ENTER HARWICH SPECIAL MILITARY AREA.**

for the purpose of _Visiting_

within the _____ **FELIXSTOWE SECTION.**

HARWICH SECTION.

1 0 NOV 1917

Until _____

unless withdrawn or otherwise determined.

P. A. Owen

Date _11 Jy 17_ Competent

Captain for Major-General
MILITARY Authority.

[For Special Conditions, if any, see overleaf.]

63/66 With the outbreak of war in August 1914 there was great concern that enemy spies and saboteurs were at work in Britain, and people with German-sounding names came under immediate suspicion. Boy Scouts were set to guarding railway bridges and similar vulnerable positions, and in Suffolk Sea Scouts were employed with the Coast Guard on watching the coast. The handbill on the opposite page warns "Don't talk. The Enemy has ears everywhere." Along the coast and in the vicinity of ports there were prohibited areas, and it was necessary to have a permit from the military authorities if one needed to enter such areas either on business or to visit one's friends; a permit issued to an Ipswich resident is illustrated above, while below is a pass issued to a railway engine driver allowing him to operate on the line between Felixstowe Town station and the Beach station.

PASS.

Name _H. Hagger_

Address _Ipswich_

has permission until further order ~or from~

_____ to _____ to pass

through the Outposts by Day ~night~ between
Felixstowe & _Felixstowe Beach_

for the purpose of _Railway Work_

Signed

Frankland

PEEWIT COTTAGE,
1st Sept ~August~ 1914.

Captain

Provost Marshal,
Landguard Sub-Command.

67 During the war many wounded servicemen were sent to hospital in Ipswich, the East Suffolk and Ipswich Hospital receiving 7,777 casualties in the five years of war. Broadwater, a large house in Belstead Road belonging to Ipswich businessman William Paul, was turned into a war hospital, and so was Ranelagh Road School; Gippeswyk Hall became a measles hospital for soldiers. The casualties were taken from ambulance trains at Ipswich station by members of the British Red Cross and the St. John Ambulance Brigade and carried to the hospitals, while other members of the two organisations made up wound dressings and other medical necessities for use in France and other war zones. In 1917 Miss Hall, the matron of the Broadwater Hospital, was awarded the Royal Red Cross in recognition of her "patient and

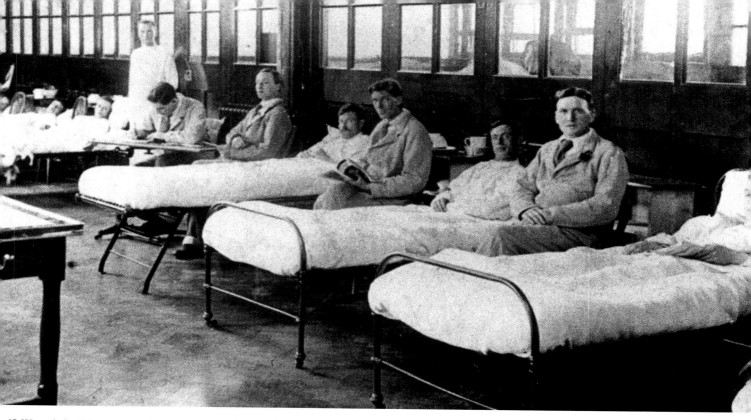

68 Wounded soldiers in one of the wards at the Ranelagh Road School war hospital. Just behind the beds is one of the glazed folding partitions that had divided one classroom from another; they could be folded back to open up the classrooms for morning assembly.

69 Schools, factories and other places produced rolls of honour naming those who had gone into the services during the war, and after the war many similar organisations erected memorials to those who had died on war service. This roll of honour from Nacton Road Council School, Ipswich, bears the names of four members of staff and more than 120 old boys who were serving in the forces; not all of them returned.

70 The *Weekly Dispatch*, a London newspaper, organised a tobacco fund to send tobacco and "smokes" to troops serving overseas, and with the supplies went a card that was to be sent back to the person contributing to the fund. This one found its way back from a Field Post Office in France to a lady at Hitcham. "In thanking the donor, please do not mention your unit" says an instruction on the card, but in a serious breach of security the recipient reveals that he is serving with the 80th Battery, Royal Field Artillery, in the 15th Brigade, British Expeditionary Force. What a breach of discipline!

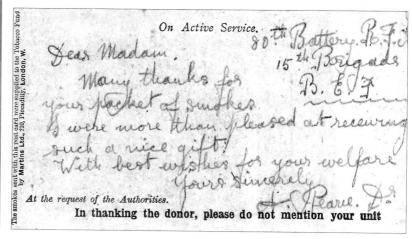

71/72 On the night of 30 April 1915 Ipswich had its first taste of attack from the air, something that was to become all too familiar not only later in the First World War but to a much greater extent in the Second. A German Zeppelin dropped a number of Goldschmidt incendiary bombs, metal cones filled with oil and bound with tarred rope. The first fell fairly harmlessly outside the Presbyterian Church on Barrack Corner, and the second fell in the roadway at the top of Waterloo Road; another set light to a house in Brooks Hall Road, and before long three houses were blazing fiercely, flames shooting up through the roof. To the people of Ipswich it was just another example of the Germans attempting to terrorise the civilian population. "If the Germans only knew that Mr. Goodwin, who is a tailor working for Mr. Barnabus Scott, was engaged in making military breeches, they would probably endeavour to justify the raid by stating that they had destroyed military stores," said the *East Anglian Daily Times* with heavy sarcasm. "Certainly the three pairs of officers' breeches which he was making were utterly destroyed. . .". The newspaper reported contemptuously that the German official communiqué had stated "Coast fortifications at Harwich were bombarded last night."

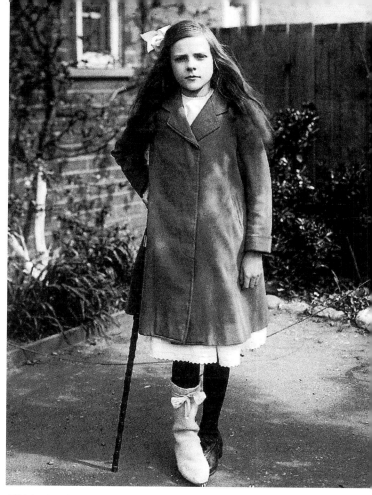

73 The Ipswich fire chief, Supt. George Galloway, with one of the bombs that fell on Ipswich in 1915.

74 Mr. Goodwin's niece Elsie seems to have received a fairly minor injury when the bomb dropped on her uncle's house, and ignited in her bedroom.

75/76 A second Zeppelin raid carried out on 31st March 1916 by the L.15 caused considerable damage to houses in Key Street, a bomb that fell at the back of the Old Custom House killing a man outside the Gun public house on the corner of Lower Orwell Street. The L.15 went on to attack London, but was hit first by anti-aircraft fire and then by the bullets of a night fighter, with the result that it crashed into the sea off the Essex coast. The Zeppelin's crew were picked up by naval ships. These views show the damage caused; a soldier billeted in the house lost a leg in the bombing.

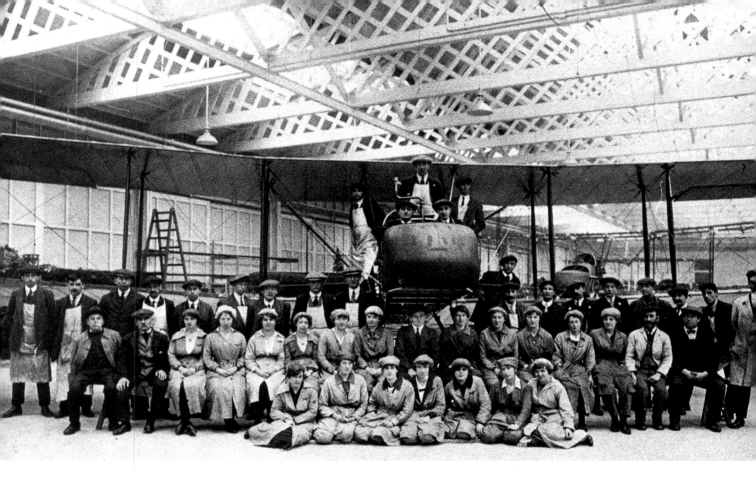

77/78 Such was the demand for aircraft for the Royal Flying Corps during the First World War that engineering companies in different parts of the country were asked to produce aeroplanes of various designs. At Ipswich Ransomes Sims & Jefferies began to build aircraft in hangars erected in what had been the claypit of a brickworks in Fore Hamlet. The first aircraft to be built there were FE.2b fighters with the engine set behind the pilot in a nacelle, one of which is seen above in the "White City", as the works became known, with those who were employed on this job, the majority of them women. Below, work is proceeding on the making of wing sections for these planes. Besides building several hundred FE.2b fighters Ransomes also made 400 of the Airco D.H.6 aircraft, known to pilots as the "Widow Maker" because of their unsavoury reputation. Ransomes were to have built the Vickers Vimy bomber (an example of which became the first aeroplane to fly the Atlantic from west to east in 1919), but with the coming of peace orders both for the FE.2b and the Vimy were cancelled. By that time Ransomes had built no fewer than 790 aeroplanes.

79 The nacelle of an FE.2b containing gunner's position, pilot's cockpit and engine in Ransomes' works. In the background can be seen an Airco D.H.6.

80 An FE.2b built by Ransomes Sims & Jefferies. Morale at the works was boosted by the receipt in 1917 of a letter stating that the first aircraft of this type to be built by the company was involved in the shooting down of the Zeppelin L.48 at Theberton on 17 June that year.

81/82 Another Ipswich firm that was heavily involved in aircraft production between 1914 and 1918 was Frederick Tibbenham, in Turret Lane. Besides making wings and other parts for aeroplanes, possibly as sub-contractors to Ransomes, Sims & Jefferies, Tibbenham's were busy making airscrews. In the picture above a woman worker can be seen carefully planing the blade of a wooden airscrew; the unfinished propellers leaning against the wall show how they were made up of a number of laminations glued together. Large four-bladed propellers can be seen leaving the firm's works on horse-drawn waggons in the photograph below.

83 Women munitions workers in one of the workshops at Ransomes Sims & Jefferies. Following the outbreak of war 1,600 Ransomes employees joined the forces, 130 of them being killed, and their places at the workbenches and in the workshops were taken by women workers who had never had the opportunity of such employment before. The firm was making shell cases and many other such items during the war.

84 The British Diesel Company was set up in 1912 to produce the oil engines designed by Dr. Rudolf Diesel, who was on his way to visit the Ipswich factory when he disappeared from the Great Eastern Railway continental steamer *Dresden* as it sailed from Antwerp to Harwich on the night of 29-30 September 1913. The Diesel Works on land off Hadleigh Road closed in 1914 but was soon reopened by Vickers-Petters and turned to the production of engines for submarines. Royal Navy submarines were often to be seen in Ipswich Dock during the war while their engines were being overhauled by men from the Diesel Works. Ten were refitted during 1915, another 26 in 1916 and 18 the following year. The photograph shows one of the bigger engines built at the Ipswich works, a 12-cylinder solid injection submarine engine.

85 A group of women workers at Ransomes during the First World War. The triangular badge that they wear on their overalls marks them as war workers, playing their part in fighting the war against Germany. In the course of the war Ransomes produced 650 aeroplane and airship hangars, 3,700 bombs, 1,000,000 steel forgings, 440,000 shell cases, 610,000 practice shot, 3,000,000 shell and fuse parts, 225 trench howitzers, 1,700 mines, 1,500 mine sinkers and 10,000 mortar bombs as well as a vast range of ploughs and agricultural equipment to help boost home food production.

86 One of the electric trucks made by Ransomes Sims & Jefferies loaded with munitions made at the firm's Orwell Works, apparently for a display or procession.

87 Soldiers and war workers posing around a steam traction engine, perhaps while taking part in one of the savings drives held during the war. The building in the background belongs to William Brown & Co. (Ipswich) Ltd., who were important timber merchants with premises in various parts of the dock area.

88 One of the advantages enjoyed by certain of the Ipswich engineering factories was the facility for sending their products away by railway. This goods train, headed by Great Eastern Railway class T18 tank engine No. 292, is leaving the lower yard at Ipswich with twenty General Service wagons made for the Army Service Corps in 1915, having most likely just crossed the Bridge Street crossing close to Stoke Bridge from the dock tramway that ran alongside the firm's Orwell Works. The construction of horse-drawn wagons was just one contribution made by Ipswich firms to the war effort; Ransomes made 5,000 of them between 1914 and 1918.

89 Large shells made by Ransomes & Rapier Ltd. at Waterside Works are to the fore in the Government Inspection Department, where all the thousands of shells produced were checked.

90 Another view of the Government Inspection Department, with many of the women workers employed in wartime by Ransomes & Rapier.

91 Shells stacked in the Storing and Cleaning Department.

92 As more and more men joined the services, women were brought in to take their place. At Ransomes, Tibbenhams and in other places they worked on munitions and stitched aeroplane fabric, and on the Ipswich Corporation Tramways they worked as tram conductresses. The "clippies", as they were soon termed, helped to keep the transport services running as wartime conditions provided more and more problems. Traffic superintendent Arthur Butler joined some of the "clippies" and the remaining tram drivers for this group photograph outside the depot in Constantine Road. A close look at the tram on the right reveals that the single headlamp has been masked so that only a tiny spot of light shall show to dilute the blackout. However, arcing between the trolley arm and the overhead wires often contravened the blackout regulations, but nothing could be done about that.

93 Another group of conductoresses outside the tram sheds. When the war was over the women were no longer wanted, and the "clippies" and munitions workers were all discharged. Even more unhappily, many of their male colleagues returning from "the War to end all Wars" also soon found themselves out of work.

94/96 Children of Springfield Road School in various forms of fancy dress taking part in a savings drive. Raising money for the war effort was a vita part of life at home, and the leaflet below left urges people to buy National War Bonds that would be repaid from 1922 onwards. The leaflet below right urging people to buy War Bonds and War Savings Certificates was dropped by aeroplane over Ipswich in 1918, during a "Destroyer Week" which raised £431,138.

BARCLAYS BANK
LIMITED.
IPSWICH.

ISSUE OF
NATIONAL WAR BONDS

£5 % **BONDS.** Repayable 1st October, 1922, at 102 % ;

£5 % **BONDS.** Repayable 1st October, 1924, at 103 % ;

£5 % **BONDS.** Repayable 1st October, 1927, at 105 % ;

AND

£4 % **BONDS.** Repayable 1st October, 1927, at 100 % .
("Income Tax Compounded.")

Interest payable half-yearly on the 1st APRIL and 1st OCTOBER.

First Dividend payable 1st APRIL, 1918.

PRICE OF ISSUE £100 PER CENT.

PAYABLE ON APPLICATION.

THE GOVERNOR & COMPANY OF THE BANK OF ENGLAND are authorized by the Lords Commissioners of His Majesty's Treasury to receive on the 2nd October, 1917, and thereafter until further notice, applications for the above Bonds. Applications may be lodged at any Office of the Banks hereafter mentioned.

The Principal and Interest of the Bonds are chargeable on the Consolidated Fund of the United Kingdom.

Bonds of this issue, and the interest payable from time to time in respect thereof, will be exempt from all British taxation, present or future, if it is shown in the manner directed by the Treasury that they are in the beneficial ownership of a person who is neither domiciled nor ordinarily resident in the United Kingdom of Great Britain and Ireland.

Further, the interest payable from time to time in respect of £5 per cent. Bonds of this issue will be exempt from British Income Tax, present or future, if it is shown in the manner directed by the Treasury that the Bonds are in the beneficial ownership of a person who is not ordinarily resident in the United Kingdom of Great Britain and Ireland, without

7. 3. 18

IPSWICH
DESTROYER
Will YOU Help?
BUY
War Bonds
AND
War Savings
Certificates.

THIS BILL WAS DROPPED FROM AN AEROPLANE OVER IPSWICH

97/98 "Your country needs You!" declared Lord Kitchener on that most famous of recruiting posters, and thousands of Suffolk men answered the call by the man they considered to be one of them. The younger men volunteered for the Army, "Kitchener's Army", and those who were too old for overseas service joined the Volunteer Training Corps, while some skilled men were retained to keep the engineering factories running. Above is the band of the Suffolk Volunteer Training Corps, later the 1st Volunteer Battalion Suffolk Regiment, and the group below is of the men of Witnesham and district who served in one capacity or another in the First World War.

99 Two C-class submarines, early craft built in 1906 by Vickers at Barrow-in-Furness, alongside HMS *Ganges II* at Shotley. These and other later submarines, including many of the E-class, operated from Harwich harbour with considerable success during the First World War. Two of the older boats, C.1 and C.3, were employed in the daring Zeebrugge raid of 23 April 1918, the C.3 being driven under a viaduct and blown up to prevent German reinforcements passing over the viaduct to reach the Mole; her commanding officer in that operation, Lieut. Richard Sandford, was awarded the Victoria Cross for most conspicuous gallantry.

100 A number of the Harwich submarines were lost during the war, including E.4 which was running submerged off Harwich, in 1916, when it collided with E.41 travelling on the surface. Both boats sank with heavy loss of life. Crew members of the lost submarines are buried in the naval cemetery behind Shotley Church, in a corner of the cemetery reserved for submariners.

·SURRENDERED·
·GERMAN·
·SUBMARINES·
·IN·
·HARWICH·
·HARBOUR· 21.11.18.

101/102 After the signing of the Armistice on 11 November 1918, arrangements were made for German U-boats to be surrendered at Harwich, and it fell to the ships of Harwich Force under Commodore Reginald Tyrwhitt to escort the first 20 U-boats into the harbour on 20th November. They were followed by many others in succeeding weeks, until there were no fewer than 150 submarines moored in the River Stour. Precautions were taken on board the British warships to ensure that the German crews did not attempt to scuttle their boats on the way in.

103 There was great rejoicing in Ipswich when the war came to an end. News of the signing of the Armistice reached Ransomes' Orwell Works by telephone at 9.30 on the morning of 11 November, and the works closed at 11.30, the employees nevertheless being paid for the full day. News of the Armistice was greeted by the sounding of factory hooters and buzzers, and the town was soon decorated with flags and bunting. Many people gathered on Cornhill to celebrate the end of hostilities. More formal celebrations had to wait until July the following year when the peace treaty was signed. The upper picture shows a packed crowd on Cornhill, apparently being held back by just two burly policemen of the Borough Police Force. Austen, Eddy, Harold and Basil were there, according to the writing on the card. The South African War memorial can be seen on the extreme left.

104 In the lower picture a pipe band belonging to a Scottish regiment stationed in the area leads the way out of Northgate towards Christchurch Park for the peace celebrations of July, 1919. Clearing the way are two policemen. There were light showers during the day, but Ipswich escaped the heavy rain that marred the celebrations in some parts of the country. Six guns of the 126th Battery Royal Field Artillery stationed at Warren Heath, where the Sainsbury supermarket now stands, fired a 21-gun salute at midday. As the last shot was fired the band of the 1st Suffolk Volunteer Regiment (formerly the Volunteer Training Corps) struck up the National Anthem, following it with the regimental march "Speed the Plough".

105/106 According to a contemporary newspaper report "By two o'clock a steady stream of people were converging to Christchurch Park from all points of the compass", and a huge crowd in the park watched the celebrations, which included a somewhat spectacular swimming display at the Round Pond put on by members of the Ipswich Swimming Club. In preparation for the swimming Mr. H.L. Cooke, who had oyster rooms in Market Lane, off the Buttermarket, lent an oyster dredge, a reminder of the one-time Orwell oyster fishery, to clear the pond of old tins and other rubbish.

107 The need for savings was no less after the war, as one of the banners being carried in the Victory Loan procession indicates. The Victory tableau is carried on one of the Ipswich-built battery electric lorries with the Ipswich registration DX-1813; two of these are preserved in the Ipswich Transport Museum. From Barrack Corner the procession went along Westgate Street and across Cornhill, along Tavern Street and Carr Street, down "the Wash" (Upper Orwell Street) and through Orwell Place and Tacket Street into Upper Brook Street and along the Buttermarket and so back to the Cornhill. While the decorated vehicles drove off down Princes Street those people who had walked in the procession paused on Cornhill "to listen to a few brief speeches".

108 These youngsters from Springfield Road School put on a colourful tableau for the Victory Loan procession on 5 July 1919. They are seen here in Kingston Road, off Bramford Lane. The Victory Loan Week raised £870,870.

109 Ipswich was visited by two Lanchester armoured cars on 11 July 1919 as part of a campaign to boost savings in the town. The vehicles, which were said by the *East Anglian Daily Times* to be the last of 36 built in the early days of the war, had been to Norwich, Southwold and Woodbridge on the way to Ipswich. A special bank was opened for the week at the Town Hall, staffed by cashiers from the various banks in the town, to take contributions to the Victory Loan.

110 A civic reception at the Town Hall was accorded to the cadre of the 4th Battalion Suffolk Regiment on 11th October 1919. The battalion, which in peacetime was a Territorial Army battalion, had gone to war in November 1914, returned to this country in August after more than four years overseas, and was due for demobilisation. The officers are seen here on the Town Hall steps with the Mayor, Mr. Frederick Rands, and members of the Corporation.

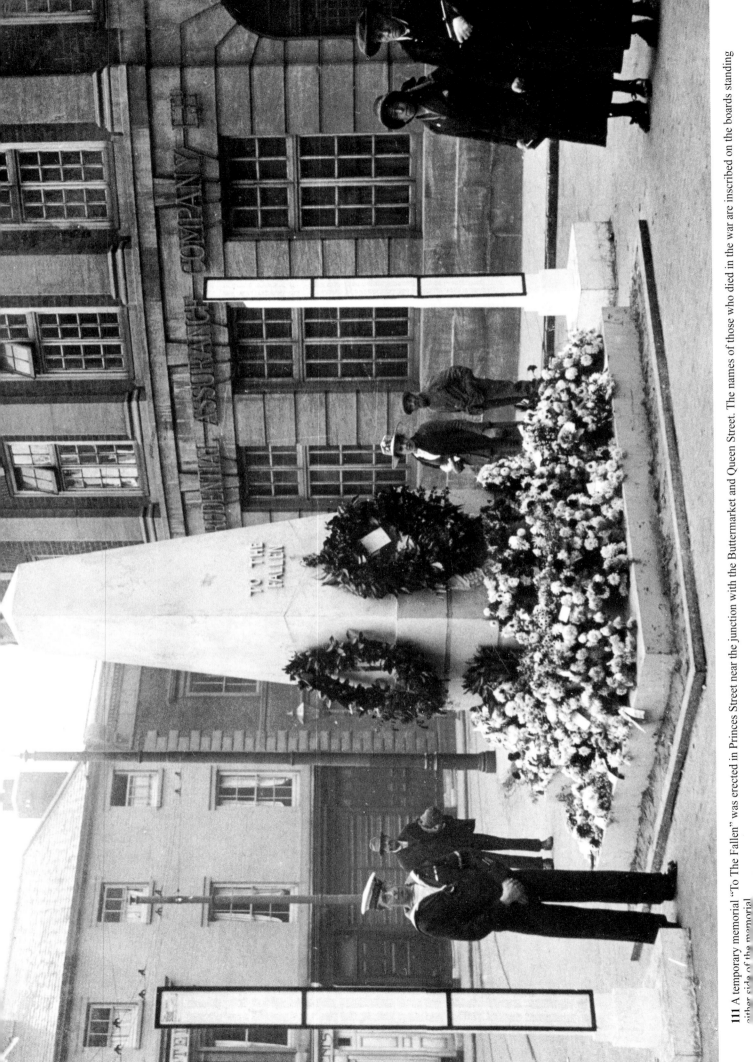

111 A temporary memorial "To The Fallen" was erected in Princes Street near the junction with the Buttermarket and Queen Street. The names of those who died in the war are inscribed on the boards standing either side of the memorial.

112 Various events were organised to raise money for the Ipswich war memorial, and one of them was a fete on 6 August 1919. Decorated motor-cycles and cycles were one of the attractions.

113 Some 10,000 Ipswich men served in the Forces during the First World War, and the names of 1,481 who died in the conflict were inscribed on the war memorial that was erected in Christchurch Park and dedicated on 3 May 1924. The Ipswich War Memorial Fund raised some £50,000, of which only £5,000 was spent on the Christchurch Park memorial, the rest being used to build an extension to the East Suffolk and Ipswich Hospital in Anglesea Road. The war memorial wing was erected on the former Militia Depot site to the west of the hospital.

114/115 In the 1920s Ipswich had a number of Royal Artillery Territorial units with drill halls in Woodbridge Road and Great Gipping Street, and it seems likely that they might have used the Barracks for training. The picture above of a howitzer and its crew probably shows a Territorial unit; the limber carrying the ammunition is in the left background. Below are horses and grooms; the horses had not at that time been replaced by mechanical haulage.

116 The 1st Battalion The Suffolk Regiment performed a recruiting march around Suffolk in the summer of 1927, leaving Meeanee Barracks at Colchester on 16 August and camping for the night at Stratford St. Mary before marching on to Ipswich the next day. The picture shows the Corps of Drums and the regimental band, in service dress rather than the scarlet tunics of earlier years, leading the battalion on to the Cornhill. After Trooping the Colour in Christchurch Park the battalion stayed the night at Ipswich Barracks and then attended a lunch hosted by the Mayor in the Corn Exchange, followed later in the day by a tattoo and sports in Christchurch Park. The battalion left Ipswich on 19 August to march to Stowmarket, and then on succeeding days to Bury St. Edmunds, Sudbury and back to Colchester.

117 Kaiser Wilhelm made the mistake of calling the regular soldiers who were first in the field in France in 1914 "this contemptible little army". Part of that army was the 2nd Battalion The Suffolk Regiment, which during the retreat from Mons made a very gallant stand at Le Cateau, preventing the Germans from sweeping on towards Paris but losing 720 men killed, wounded or missing. After the war the survivors of the expeditionary force formed their own organisation, which they called the Old Contemptibles. In the photograph below, taken by H. Walters & Son, of 11 St. Margaret's Plain, the Ipswich branch of the Old Contemptibles parade their Standard in Derby Road about 1928-30.

118 From the time the Government took over the heath during the First World War, the air station at Martlesham Heath played a very significant part in the development of aviation. It was commissioned as a Royal Flying Corps station in January 1917 and became the home of the Aircraft Testing Flight when that unit moved from RAF Martlesham Heath, and in 1924 the Aircraft Testing Flight was joined by the Armament Experimental Flight, which had at one time been at Orfordness. From 1924 the station was the Aeroplane and Armament Experimental Establishment, and from then until the A & AEE moved at the outbreak of the Second World War every land-based aircraft that entered service with the RAF came to Martlesham Heath for evaluation. Civilian aircraft came to the station to be tested for their certificate of airworthiness. One of the early ventures was the development of aerial photography, both for the taking of reconnaissance photographs for the use of the army on the ground and for use in the other experiments being carried on at the station, including investigations into the trajectory of bombs dropped from aircraft. The picture shows members of the Photographic Flight in 1919, including four women.

119 A group of officers at Martlesham Heath standing in front of a Handley Page V/1500, the RAF's first four-engined bomber. On the left is Captain Walden Hammond, of the Photographic Flight, who took some of the earliest photographs from the air. Although too late to see action in the First World War, the V/1500 made history by making the first through flight from England to India; leaving Martlesham Heath on 13 December 1918, a V/1500 named HMA *Carthusian* flew to Karachi by way of Rome, Malta, Cairo and Baghdad, arriving in India early in January 1919. It is probably that aircraft that appears in the photograph.

120 The car seen in this picture at Martlesham Heath would certainly not have got its owner to India, but no doubt it took him and his fellow officers into Ipswich in some style.

121 The Officers' Mess was a long hut-like building with a verandah along one side. In this view of the interior it appears somewhat spartan, but here were gathered some of the finest pilots and the most experienced technical officers in the service. Some of the Martlesham test pilots joined aircraft manufacturing companies when they left the RAF and continued to play an important part in the test-flying of new types of aircraft. Although it might have been expected that the pilots taking part in the annual Schneider Trophy air races of the 1920s and early 1930s would have come from the Marine Aircraft Experimental Establishment at Felixstowe, where much of the practice for the races was carried on, they were in fact drawn from the ranks of the Martlesham Heath test pilots.

122 The usual way of starting aircraft engines in the early days was to swing the propeller by hand, but in the 1920s the Hucks Starter was designed to do the same job mechanically. This Hucks Starter on a Ford Model T chassis was made by Ransomes Sims & Jefferies in Ipswich.

123 Low flying sometimes necessitated the temporary closure of the Woodbridge-Felixstowe road where it passed through the camp. A proposal to re-route the road around the aerodrome was dropped, and instead measures, including the posting of sentries to stop traffic when low flying was in progress, were taken to ensure public safety. In this photograph an Avro 504K, or possibly a 504N, is using the Aircraft Speed Range which in the 1920s crossed the road within the station; a sentry box can be seen to the left of the road, with the doors of one of the hangars at extreme left. Photography by civilians was expressly forbidden in the area of the aerodrome; the amateur photographer who took this picture had his camera and film confiscated, but they were later returned to him.

124 Two of the hangars at Martlesham Heath, a picture taken in 1923. The smaller hangar on the left was one of several reputed to have been built about 1917 by German prisoners-of-war accommodated in a camp at Woodbridge. These had Belfast-truss roofs constructed of timber.

125 The monstrous Beardmore Inflexible was assembled at Martlesham Heath, from which it made its first flight on 5 March 1928. Not only was it by far the biggest aircraft of its day but it was also one of the earliest all-metal aircraft, both the airframe and the covering of the wings and fuselage being of duralumin. Built by the Scottish engineering firm of William Beardmore, who had earlier had considerable experience of airship construction, the Inflexible represented a departure from the normal line of bomber development, being a high wing monoplane; other bombers designed for the RAF at that time were almost all biplanes. There were three engines, one in the nose and one under each wing, and two enormous landing wheels with a diameter of 7 feet 4 inches carried the 16-ton weight of this pioneer aircraft. It was during the period of testing at Martlesham Heath that the Inflexible made an impressive appearance at the Hendon Air Show in 1928. The trials carried out showed that this aircraft, which was much ahead of its time, was so heavy that it was unable to carry any worthwhile bomb load. Eventually the wings were taken off and placed at the side of B Flight hangar, where they were left for some years to assess the effect of weathering on the metal structure. Although not a success in itself, the Inflexible helped to pave the way for the four-engined heavy bombers of the Second World War.

126 The RAF's first parachute section was formed at Martlesham Heath commanded by Flight Lieutenant John Potter, inventor of the Potter parachute. Sergeant Hawking, MM, Corporal East and ten men known as 'Loonies' assisted him. In the photograph we see an early type of parachute worn by a DH 9A pilot clearly showing the static line used to open the parachute.

127 below: Staff of the Flight Testing Section and Armourers in front of Handley Page Harrow K.6934 in B Flight hangar in 1937. The Harrow, one of the new generation of monoplane twin-engined bombers entering service with the RAF in the late 1930s, was evaluated by both the Performance Testing Section and the Armament Testing Section at Martlesham Heath in 1937-38.

28 The very latest types destined to see service with the RAF were lined up for royal inspection on 8 July 1936 when King Edward VIII and his brother, the Duke of York (to be crowned the following year as King George VI), visited Martlesham Heath. The King showed a particular interest in the prototype Supermarine Spitfire, K5054, climbing up to inspect the cockpit as seen in the photograph above. The designer of the Spitfire, R.J. Mitchell, is at the right of the party ahead of the port wing.

29 The King and his brother also inspected the prototype Westland Lysander K6127, an army co-operation aircraft that during the Second World War was used on clandestine operations in connection with the Resistance in Occupied Europe. Both the royal brothers and the senior officers accompanying them were wearing black armbands; King George V had died only a short time before their visit.

130/131 Strange things were going on at Bawdsey Manor in the 1930s, and there was talk locally of death rays and of rays that stopped car engines and other internal combustion motors. The Manor, which had been built by Sir Cuthbert Quilter as a family home, was bought by the Air Ministry in 1936 for Sir Robert Watson-Watt's team of scientists who had been working at Orfordness on a new system for warning of approaching aircraft. By 1939 the grounds of the Manor housed the first Chain Home radar station, soon to be part of a series of stations around the coast that would play a vital part in the Battle of Britain and subsequent air operations. Many of those who served at Bawdsey Manor during the war were members of the Women's Auxiliary Air Force, a group of whom can be seen below.

132 While radio-location, later renamed radar, was being developed at Orfordness and later at Bawdsey Manor, the RAF station at Martlesham Heath was home to a Radar Development Flight operating aircraft that co-operated with the team experimenting with the new equipment. In the picture above, taken in 1938 or 1939, members of the Radar Development Flight line up in front of a Fairey Battle light bomber employed in the experimental operations. Air Chief Marshal Sir Hugh Dowding, chief of Fighter Command, flew in an aircraft of this type fitted with the early Air Interception radar when he paid a visit to Martlesham Heath in July 1939.

133 As development of radar progressed the first operational AI radars were installed in Bristol Blenheim Mk.I night fighters similar to that seen below. In this picture certain of the AI radar aerials have been removed by the censor, but those above and below the port wing remain; there are other copies of the same photograph in which these have also disappeared. In order to account for the success of RAF night fighters fitted with the early AI sets the story was spread that night fighter pilots were being fed large quantities of carrots to improve their night sight. A particularly successful night fighter pilot, Group Captain John Cunningham, who was given the nickname of "Cat's-eyes" by the press, has said that the advent of Ground Controlled Interception combined with AI was the turning point in night fighter operations.

134 The fall of France in June 1940 and the extrication of a not-inconsiderable part of the British Expeditionary Force from the beaches of Dunkirk left Britain under the threat of imminent attack. Already on 14 May the Secretary of State for War, Anthony Eden, had announced the formation of Local Defence Volunteers, and by the end of the month some 300,000 men had joined, though few of them had proper uniforms or adequate arms at that time. At the end of July the rapidly-expanding force received a new name, the Home Guard. As time went on this citizen army received both uniforms and arms, and in August Suffolk units were formally affiliated to the Suffolk Regiment and were permitted to wear the Castle and Key of Gibraltar badge of the regiment, as do these men of J Company of the 9th Suffolk Battalion, formed from the workforce of the engineering firm of E.R.& F. Turner. On the formation in 1942 of the 11th Battalion the Turner unit became the new battalion's C Company.

135 The officer commanding D Company, 11th Suffolk Battalion, Major J.B. Webster, and his officers. Major Webster was originally in command of the works platoon at Cranes in Nacton Road, which became C Platoon of D Company responsible for defending the perimeter of the town from the northern boundary of Ipswich Airport to Felixstowe Road. Major Webster took command of the company on the death of Major W.J. Rice, the original C.O. When the "invasion imminent" signal was received on 7 September 1940 all the volunteers were called out and the company positions were manned, rifles and ammunition being issued indiscriminately to the men. It is said that it took months for the quartermaster to get his books straight again after that night.

136 The officers of C Company of the 9th Suffolk Battalion, which was formed in 1940 as the Ipswich battalion. When the battalion strength reached 3,000 men in the summer of 1942 it was decided to form an 11th Battalion with headquarters at the drill hall in Woodbridge Road under Lieut.-Col. H.C. Howes, who had taken a prominent part in the activities of the 9th Battalion. Standing, left to right, are Lieut. F.E. Schur, Lieut. A.E. Catling, Lieut. A.C. Mayell, Lieut. J.W. Hatfield, Capt. H.C. Garnham, Lieut. A.S. Stokes, Lieut. P.C. Mumford, Lieut. H. Pillar, and Lieut. E. Barnard. Sitting are Lieut. J. Miles, Lieut. K.M. Mellonie, Lieut. R.A. Horsley, Major H. Norwood, Lieut. R. Chambers and C.S.M. P. Howell.

137 The Home Guard was also active in the country districts around Ipswich. This photograph shows volunteers from Swilland, Witnesham and Helmingham about 1944. Standing at the back are, left to right, unknown, "Tubby" Whiting, Albert Whiting, George Whitelaw, Geoff Threadkell, Geoff Thurlow, "Stud" Potter, Sid Jordan and "Sporley" Wells. In the middle row are Jack Woods, unknown, Bill Rookyard, unknown, Ray Runnacles, "Sonny" Nunn, Ben Last and Ted Taylor. Sitting at the front are Doug Cotton, Percy Ramsey, Lewis James, John Mayhew, Lieut. Hitchcock, unknown, Clem Styles, Harold Hammond and John Styles.

138 One of the weapons with which the Home Guard was equipped was the spigot mortar, an anti-tank mortar of dubious effectiveness. In the picture is a team from D Company of 11th Suffolk Battalion, winners of the East Suffolk Spigot Mortar Competition. The team is, left to right, S.K. Bird, G. Woolacott, H. Galpin, Cpl. G. Baker, and C. Smith. Representing the 11th Battalion, the team gained top place in spite of an accident when the second round burst the gun casing, fortunately without causing serious injury to any of the gun team.

139 Much of the equipment used by the Home Guard was improvised in one way or another. In this picture Major-General J.A. Aizlewood is being shown a Browning .300 machine gun that has been mounted for use against low-flying aircraft. The mobile mounting was designed and made at the Orwell Works of Ransomes Sims & Jefferies, which had its own Home Guard unit that became B Company of the 11th Battalion. The "brass hat's" breeches and polished boots contrast with the battledress worn by the Home Guard officers accompanying him on his inspection.

140 A Home Guard platoon drilling in the Dales brickyard, with the brick kiln in the background. The brickyard, operated by A. Bolton & Co., with its claypits and sandpits, provided a suitable environment for the Home Guard to carry out battle training, and was also used by Civil Defence units and first aid parties for some very effective exercises.

141 The officers of B Company, which originated in June 1940 as the works unit of Ransomes Sims & Jefferies. One of the unit's duties was to mount an anti-sabotage guard at Orwell Works, which during the war was producing munitions as well as agricultural machinery, the first guard being mounted on 1st July 1940. This guard continued to be mounted every night for three years, it becoming traditional that the officers of the unit provided the Christmas Eve guard.

142 The sergeants and headquarters staff of B Company, all of them employees of Ransomes Sims & Jefferies. Although the Home Guard has, perhaps as a result of the TV series "Dad's Army", come to be regarded as something of a joke, it was anything but a joke in the early 1940s when men who had been doing strenuous work in the factory donned their uniform and spent the evening in weapons training or mounted guard on the works for the night.

143 The Post Office, which controlled the telephone and telegraph services as well as the postal service, formed its own unit of the LDV in May 1940. In the early days it was known as the 2nd Post Office East Anglian Battalion, but in December 1940 it was renamed the 13th P.O. Battalion Essex Home Guard, and then in the following March it became the 13th Essex (35th G.P.O.) Battalion, with its D Company under the command of Major R.R. King at the Old Cattle Market in Ipswich. Other companies were based in Bury St. Edmunds and Saxmundham, with platoons in Sudbury and Woodbridge. The battalion's specialist duties included the provision of armed guards on telephone exchanges, repeater stations and other key buildings and the protection of working parties repairing cables. The photograph shows personnel of the Ipswich company towards the end of the war.

144 As war clouds gathered the organisation of the Air Raid Precautions service in Ipswich began in 1938, the training of the first volunteers beginning in March that year. By the outbreak of war in September 1939 no fewer than 867 air raid wardens had been enrolled, though there had been difficulties in obtaining sufficient volunteers in the centre of the town and on the new estates that had sprung up on the outskirts. Other volunteers enrolled in emergency first aid units, in the Auxiliary Fire Service and other services. This photograph, taken in August 1943, shows a mobile first aid team at Heathfields, in Woodbridge Road, outside the building that was used for training in the evenings from 6 pm to 9 pm; it was part of the Poor Law Institution, more commonly known as the Workhouse. Seated in the middle of the group is Dr. Sidney Scott, who had a surgery at the corner of Woodbridge Road and Rushmere Road.

145 The Duke of Kent inspecting members of a first aid team lined up in front of their vehicles during his visit to Ipswich. The first member of the Royal Family to work in the civil service, the Duke of Kent joined the Royal Air Force on the outbreak of war and was killed on active service when his Sunderland flying boat crashed in 1942.

146 Members of another mobile first aid team seen at the ambulance station behind the E.U.R. Tavern in Croft Street. In the background is a bus converted into a mobile first aid post and other vehicles; it will be seen that the car on the left has a mask over the headlamp to cut down the light shown during the blackout. In the middle of the front row is Dr. Burns, the Assistant Medical Officer of Health, with Gladys Frost sitting next but one to him to the right.

147 It fell to the senior officers of the Ipswich Borough Police to train the original air raid wardens, hence the presence in this group of a police inspector. The early ARP uniform consisted of a blue boiler suit with an embroidered badge on the left breast bearing the letters ARP, together with a blue beret. Wardens wore black steel helmets with a white "W" painted front and back, while those in charge of posts and groups had white helmets with the "W" in black, as can be seen in the front row. This is H Group, which was responsible for the central area of the town and the dock area.

148 Later in the war Air Raid Precautions was redesignated Civil Defence and members received much smarter blue battledress with a crowned "CD" on the left pocket, as seen in this picture taken in September 1944. In spite of the change many of those in this picture still wear the silver ARP badge in their caps. It will be noticed that by this time the service had been opened to women, and that some of the men combined service in the Home Guard with their work as wardens.

149 Members of the Ransomes & Rapier Wood Department staff outside the works canteen in 1944. In the front are four members of the Air Training Corps, which prepared youngsters for service in the Royal Air Force, and behind them are Special Constables and members of the Civil Defence. In the back row are members of the Home Guard, with on the left of the row a Fire Guard wearing the distinctively-shaped steel helmet issued to fire-watchers.

150 During and after air attacks a vital role was performed by the Rescue Squads, largely staffed by building workers and others with specialist knowledge of building construction. The Rescue Squad was originally based at the Corporation Yard in Quadling Street, but this photograph was taken towards the end of the war at California School.

151 This picture of Eric Sansom, watchroom operator at the Ipswich fire station in Bond Street, was taken at 3 am on the morning of 3 September 1939, the day war broke out.

152 Until the outbreak of war fire brigades were run on a local basis, but to meet wartime conditions the fire service was reorganised in 1941 on a countrywide basis, with a full-time National Fire Service and a part-time Auxiliary Fire Service. These men are Ipswich members of the Auxiliary Fire Service; third from left is Mr. Harold Spall.

153 Private cars as well as commercial vehicles were converted into fire appliances for the Auxiliary Fire Service. These cars with ladders attached above the roof were based at the Norwich Road garage of Bolton's (Ipswich) Ltd. on the corner of Valley Road. Interestingly, only one headlamp of each is masked; presumably it was considered essential that in the case of fire appliances the driver should be able to see where he was going.

154 When the recruitment of women for watchroom duties was first proposed some senior officers stated that "women would invariably faint at the first hint of danger, and that, therefore, no reliability could be placed on them in the control room". In spite of such opinions the Ipswich Fire Brigade employed Eileen Given when the Auxiliary Fire Service was formed at the beginning of the war. It was not very long before many more women were in uniform; these firewomen are pictured at "The Moorings" in Wherstead Road, Ipswich, in March 1944.

155 Five cheerful firewomen of B Watch at NFS Station 42, the former trolleybus depot at Priory Heath. They are, left to right, Carol Birch, Cynthia Havell, Christine Dobson, "Teddy" Coleman and Margaret Strudwick ("Wicky").

156 To make up for the shortage of proper fire appliances large numbers of wartime tenders were built and equipped to tow trailer pumps. This example is an Austin K2 fire tender supplied to the National Fire Service about 1942.

157 Firemen in some of Britain's largest cities found themselves seriously overstretched as the air attacks were intensified in 1940-41, and from time to time some of them were sent to quieter stations to enable them to recuperate. At the same time firemen from East Anglia were drafted into London to help fight the huge fires caused by the Blitz. In this picture some of the "resting" firemen are seen at Red House Park Auxiliary Fire Station, Ipswich, with Mrs. Kinsey (front, centre) and Mrs. Rayner (front, right) with whom they were lodging.

158 Firemen of the Auxiliary Fire Service gathered round their trailer pump at Ipswich. Such trailer pumps were made in large numbers by firms such as Coventry Climax and were towed into action by all kinds of adapted vehicles such as the cars seen in an earlier photograph. The windows of Sidney Dunlop's shop on the corner of Derby Road and Pearce Road, in the background, have been criss-crossed with gummed paper tape to prevent the glass from flying and causing injuries if shattered by bomb blast.

159 Lined up outside the Derby Road Garage on the corner of Pearce Road are members of the Auxiliary Fire Service, including three men who also appear in the previous picture.

60/161 Ransomes & Rapier, like many other large industrial concerns, had its own volunteer fire brigade, seen here at Waterside Works in October 1942 with their three trailer pumps. Later on, as the picture below taken in 1944 shows, the volunteer firemen received somewhat rudimentary uniforms and the three trailer pumps were augmented by a "wheelbarrow" pump, seen towards the left between two of the trailer pumps. The Waterside Works Brigade won the NFS Shield for the best all-round performance by an industrial fire brigade in September 1944.

162 Oilskin coats and trousers are the only protective clothing these members of the Auxiliary Fire Service had at the beginning of the war. On the left is Noel Kindred.

163 Men of the Ipswich gasworks fire-fighting team with their trailer pump during the war; second from left is Mick Morphew, a long-term gaswork employee. The men on each side of this picture have stirrup pumps, hand-operated pumps that could be used with one hand while the pump was held in position by one foot, leaving the other hand free to direct the hose at a fire started by an incendiary bomb. All five men wear service respirators o gas masks.

164 Fire watchers on the flat roof of Boots the Chemists at 46 Tavern Street, opposite the White Horse Hotel. Spotting the fall of incendiary bombs, which were dropped in large numbers in some of the wartime raids on British towns and cities, was an important task as it enabled the fires to be tackled before they gained a hold. On the left is Winifred Bugg and on the right Barbara Rice (later Gilson), and between them in plus-fours is George Heathcote, drug department manager.

165 County Hall in St. Helen's was the report centre for East Suffolk from which all ARP services in the eastern part of Suffolk were co-ordinated. All information on incidents in the county was sent to a centre within the building with bricked-up windows and strong wooden stanchions supporting the ceiling to avoid a collapse should County Hall be struck by a bomb. The county council staff not only did their normal work but also performed ARP duties, manning phones in the report centre whenever the alarm was sounded; they slept on the premises, rooms being converted to bathrooms, shower rooms and so on, and ate in relays at the Regent cinema across the road. This picture shows members of the county hall staff relaxing on the roof of County Hall in 1942. At the back are, left to right, Cecil Parker, Paul Oxborrow and Herbert Young, in Home Guard uniform; in front are Mollie Todd (Hyde), Betty Podd (Poole) and Olga

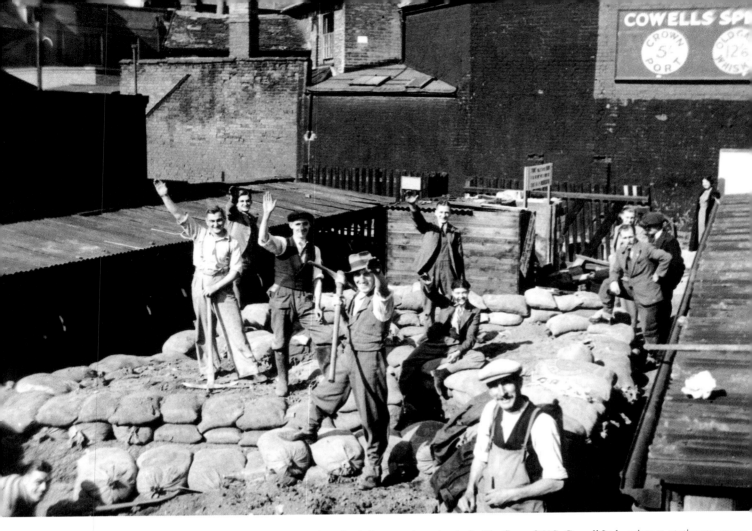

166/167 It was not only local authorities that made preparations for defence against air attack. The firm of W.S. Cowell Ltd., printers, stationers, paper and paper bag merchants, and wine merchants, in the Butter Market, with premises reaching through to Falcon Street, set to work to prepare for raids such as those that had already caused so much destruction elsewhere. Sandbags were filled and heaped up to provide shelters that it was hoped would keep staff safe from bursting bombs, those who were involved in the task clearly treating the whole thing in a somewhat lighthearted manner. The company also set up its own ARP organisation, whose members were issued with steel helmets bearing the letters "WSC" and with armbands with "ARP" and the firm's initials. Members of this organisation are seen crowded into their post, with a smiling "Charlie" Girling waving a rattle that was to be used to give warning of a gas attack, should any take place; the rattle, too, bears the initials "WSC".

168 Famous people came to entertain those who made the munitions with such shows as "Workers' Playtime". On the right is Gracie Fields, who had just taken part in a concert at Ransomes Sims & Jefferies on 14 August 1941 during an ENSA tour of England.

169 Taken from the garden of 24 Sidegate Avenue, this photograph shows the barrage balloon that operated from Ransomes' sports ground behind Sidegate Lane School, and also the earth-covered Anderson shelter that occupies part of the garden. Taking photographs of such things as barrage balloons was of course not allowed, but this was ostensibly a portrait of David Cook, and anyway the film was not developed until after the war.

170 A line of YMCA "tea cars" in Fonnereau Road outside the Young Women's Christian Association hostel and club. Although clearly labelled YMCA it does appear that the crews are all women, presumably members of the YWCA. The vehicles, used to provide refreshments for servicemen at railway stations and on isolated gun sites and similar places, are all conversions from cars or light vans.

171/172 The Borough Police Force was expanded by the recruitment of Special Constables, and also by enrolling young members of the Air Training Corps and other pre-service organisations as messengers; their role would be to keep communications open if the telephone service was disrupted by bombing. This group of men in blue are from the Norwich Road sub-station, known to those who were based there as "The Box"; the building had been a tennis pavilion. The senior officer in the front row is probably the Chief Constable, Mr. Charles J. Cresswell. Another group of Special Constables is seen below; in this case the messengers include two Sea Cadets as well as ATC cadets.

173 A constable at work in the Norwich Road sub-station control. The main police station was at the side of the Town Hall, but in wartime the town was divided into a number of sub-areas so that the bombing of one station was less likely to lead to a breakdown of policing.

174 The fact that Ipswich was a naval base throughout the Second World War is reflected in the variety of uniforms to be seen among the spectators at this parade of Special Constables. The "Specials" all wear their respirator haversacks slung over their right shoulder; gas masks had to be carried at all times by civilians as well as Servicemen as it was felt that the Germans might well launch a sudden gas attack against towns such as Ipswich.

175 Many troops were stationed around Ipswich, some of them being given the task of defending the town against air attack. These are men of 469 Search Light Company of Essex Fortress Royal Engineers, 74th Regiment, 29th Brigade, 6th AA Division, sited behind the Shepherd and Dog at Nacton in 1940. Although they have been issued with battledress or denim fatigues three of the men in the picture above proudly retain the peaked caps which they would have acquired in peacetime as Territorial Army soldiers.

176 The question mark on the "Fairyland" sign indicates what the men thought of their tented accommodation at Nacton. They were apparently prepared to make the best of it as they made friends with Sally, a spaniel belonging to the publican of the Shepherd and Dog, Mr. Walter Stalley.

177 Two 12-inch howitzers on railway carriages were stationed on the Felixstowe branch line from November 1940 to November 1942, one of them being in the yard of Orwell station and the other on a specially laid siding near the Stratton Hall level crossing. They were manned by No. 9 Super Heavy Battery, Royal Artillery, whose job was to engage any enemy warships in the approaches to Harwich Harbour. In the picture above the Stratton Hall gun is seen in its purpose-built shed, the roof of which could be rolled back when the gun was to be fired. The curving siding in the foreground is covered with camouflage netting to render it invisible to reconnaissance aircraft.

178 Neville Chamberlain arrived back from Munich waving his scrap of paper, but sensible precautions went ahead, including the provision of gas masks for the civilian population. It was feared that if war did come the Germans might make use of poison gas, and part of the equipment of the Air Raid Precautions organisation was the rattle with which to warn people of such an attack. In this picture the office staff of the Inland Revenue, Ipswich 1st District, in Providence Street are being fitted with their gas masks.

179/180 On the night of 21 June 1940 three people were killed when the first bomb to be dropped in Ipswich scored a direct hit on a house in Dale Hall Lane. It was the first of more than fifty attacks on the town. Although in the view above the house looks relatively unharmed, the other side was completely devastated, the back wall being blown out and the roof collapsing into the house, as can be seen below. A chimney stack fell in one piece and remained leaning against the building.

181 A fireman damps down the wreckage of a Dornier Do.17 that crashed into Gippeswyk Park at 6.25 pm on 21 August 1940 after being fired at by a Hawker Hurricane of No.56 Squadron piloted by Flying Officer R.E.P. Brooker. The Dornier's crew of four escaped by parachute, landing on the roof of Cocksedge's works, where they had to remain until firemen brought up ladders to rescue them. No doubt they were relieved to have landed on the roof, from which they looked down at women from the nearby houses brandishing kitchen knives and carving knives.

182/183 One of the most devastating weapons dropped from the air was the parachute mine, similar to those laid in the shipping lanes off the east coast and in the Orwell to destroy shipping. One of these landed in a stonemason's yard in the Cemetery Road area of Ipswich on 21 September 1940 but fortunately it did not explode properly. Even so, it destroyed one house and badly damaged another 25. A Royal Navy mine disposal team was brought in to deal with the mine, but it was in such a precarious condition that they decided the only thing to do was to detonate it where it lay after the residents of the whole area had been evacuated. The resulting explosion left a crater 25 feet deep, destroyed 75 houses and damaged a great many more. These two photographs show some of the devastation near the junction of Cemetery Road and Suffolk Road after the mine had been detonated.

184 On the same day that the mine landed in Cemetery Road another mine exploded on the Rushmere Heath golf course, wrecking this house in Woodbridge Road East and the Austin car that stood in the garden. The occupant of the house, Mrs. M. Woodbine, was trapped in her Anderson shelter.

185 A boy was killed when this house in Bloomfield Street, off Spring Road, was demolished by a bomb on 4 November 1940. Later that month, on the 28th, Ipswich experienced its longest "alert" of the war; it lasted for 10 hours 20 minutes.

186 The Italian air force took part in the onslaught on Britain in 1940, but with singularly little success. Of the ten bombers and forty fighters that se
out on a daylight raid on 11 November six aircraft failed to return to their bases in Belgium, including this Fiat BR20 bomber which crashed a
Bromeswell, near Woodbridge, after being engaged by Hurricanes from Martlesham Heath and elsewhere. The Italian aircraft's port engine has ende
up facing the way it has come.

187 Another of the Italian aircraft that failed to return was this Fiat CR42 biplane fighter which made a forced landing on the shingle at Orfordness, an area which was for many years home to secret research establishments. Early trials that led to the development of radar were carried out there before Robert Watson-Watt and his scientists moved to Bawdsey Manor in 1936. This CR42 is now an exhibit at the Royal Air Force Museum at Hendon.

188 As in the First World War, Ipswich engineering firms recruited many women workers when they turned to the production of munitions and other war materials. These female inspectors at Ransomes Sims & Jefferies are checking bomb parts made at Orwell Works.

189 Young women at Ransomes were trained to use welding equipment; here they are working on mine sinkers and other parts. No man was allowed to be employed on a job that a woman or a less able man could do.

190 Women workers at Ransomes were employed on such delicate jobs as filing the corners of teeth for Rolls-Royce Merlin engine timing gear.

191/192 Not all those who rallied to the call could be brought into the Ipswich factories, so Ransomes formed village groups to produce small parts for ploughs and other agricultural implements, and for electric trucks. The first was at Playford, followed by others at Waldringfield, Grundisburgh and Rushmere St. Andrew. Both in the village groups and in the Ipswich works women played a vital role, doing everything from assembling plough drawbars to the delicate machining of keyways.

193 Women workers at the Princes Street garage of Mann, Egerton & Co. A notice on the wall reads "In this war it all depends on you!"

194 A 17-pounder anti-tank gun in the Engine Works assembly shops. During the war 345 carriages for the 17-pounder were made there, as well as 400 limbers for the 17-pounder and thousands of spare parts for the guns, to say nothing of hundreds of thousands of tank components, sinker assemblies for naval mines and electric trucks, some of which were sent to Russia.

195 A long line of 25-pounder gun limbers leaving the lawnmower works, in which aircraft had been built for the Royal Flying Corps during the First World War. In the background are some of the underground air raid shelters provided for the workers.

196 When the invasion of Europe was planned one of the most vital tasks was creating safe passage through minefields which had been laid by the Germans to prevent men and vehicles from leaving the landing beaches. A number of Churchill tanks were fitted out as AVREs (Armoured Vehicle Royal Engineers) with special equipment such as this device, largely designed and produced by Ransomes Plough Works to plough a way through the minefields.

97 In October 1940 Ransomes Sims & Jefferies established a training school in which workers, some of them recruited under the Women's Industrial ational Service scheme, were trained as machinists, fitters and inspectors. During the war years more than 500 adult trainees, both men and women, assed through the school. This group of women is typical of those who were employed at Ransomes during the war. It will be noticed that many of em wear trousers; the wearing of trousers by women had been unknown, even unthinkable, before the war.

98 Although much of the works was turned over to producing weapons and munitions, Ransomes Plough Works continued to make ploughs to aid e drive to increase home food production and to bring more and more agricultural land into use. The company succeeded in reaching an output gure 50 per cent in excess of pre-war with fewer workers, of whom a very large percentage were women. This picture shows the 30,000th Motrac ough coming off the production line on 22 October 1945.

199/201 Not all the bombs that fell on Ipswich exploded, fortunately. The three photographs on this page show the recovery of a very large bomb that was dropped by a Heinkel He.111 on 7 January 1941. It fell in soft ground in Holywells Park and was dug out and defused by a bomb disposal team of the Royal Engineers. This delicate and extremely dangerous work led to the death of many of those engaged in it, though this was one of the successful operations. The casing of this bomb was almost 8ft. long and more than 2ft. in diameter, and was subsequently displayed in Christchurch Park.

202/203 At least 13 high explosive bombs were dropped in the dock area during a raid on the night of 9/10 April 1941. In the photograph above a number of vehicles, including a Ford Prefect, can be seen inside a bomb-damaged warehouse, and in the photograph below a National Fire Service fire float is being raised after being sunk in the dock during the raid; the Old Custom House can be seen in the background.

204/205 Bombs fell in Cliff Road not far from the gasworks, as seen in the picture above, and also on Cliff Quay, below. The camouflage paintin has not saved the elevator from damage. In the left background can be seen two of the armed patrol trawlers based at HMS *Bunting*, as Cliff Qua was known to the Royal Navy. On the right can be seen the spars of a spritsail barge.

206 This Dornier Do.17 bomber was forced down at Wickhambrook in West Suffolk on 23 August 1941, the crew of five being captured. It was later taken on a tour of the region for public inspection, and is seen here on display in Christchurch Park, Ipswich. The capture of a machine so relatively undamaged was a gift for the air intelligence service, who were able to discover a great deal about enemy aircraft and their equipment from a detailed inspection of the captured aircraft.

207 Altogether there were 1,165 alerts during nearly six years of war, and there were 55 actual attacks on the town, 13 of which occurred without the alert being sounded. This was the damage caused to the heat treatment shops of the Ransome Plough Works by a bomb in March 1941. Because of the effect of the repeated alerts on production in the town's factories many firms posted spotters on the roofs and a system of "crash warnings" was operated to give warning of imminent attack, workers only taking shelter on hearing the "crash warning", a warble from the air raid siren.

208 Women played their part on the land, helping to gather in the crops and to feed the population in wartime. Many young women, some of them quite unused to country life, served in the Women's Land Army. These are Molly, on the left, and Enid on a Fordson tractor.

209 Edna, otherwise known as "Titch", Rose, Pat and Joyce at work on the farm, and obviously enjoying the experience.

210 Members of the Women's Land Army parade along Crown Street by the junction to High Street. Each section holds signs indicating where they were based. This is possibly part of the county rally in August 1943 when 600 Land Girls paraded past Lord and Lady Woolton.

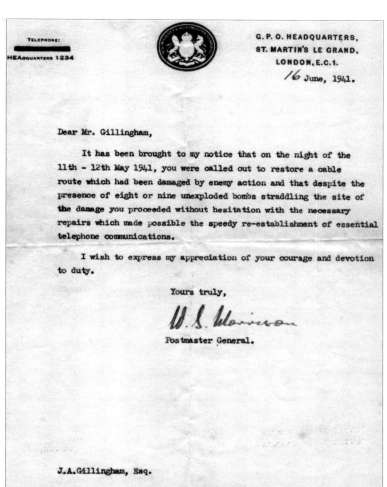

TELEPHONE:
HEADQUARTERS 1234

G.P.O. HEADQUARTERS,
ST. MARTIN'S LE GRAND,
LONDON, E.C.1.

16 June, 1941.

Dear Mr. Gillingham,

It has been brought to my notice that on the night of the 11th - 12th May 1941, you were called out to restore a cable route which had been damaged by enemy action and that despite the presence of eight or nine unexploded bombs straddling the site of the damage you proceeded without hesitation with the necessary repairs which made possible the speedy re-establishment of essential telephone communications.

I wish to express my appreciation of your courage and devotion to duty.

Yours truly,

W. S. Morrison

Postmaster General.

J.A.Gillingham, Esq.

211/212 Leslie Gillingham in his telegram boy's uniform standing by the Anderson shelter in the back garden of his home. His father John had joined the General Post Office in 1924 as a telephone engineer; on the right is a letter signed by the Postmaster General, Mr W.S.Morrison, commending him for his action in restoring telephone communications after an air raid in spite of there being a number of unexploded bombs in the vicinity.

213 To meet wartime needs a Petroleum Board was set up to take over the work of nine major distributing companies and to ensure that supplies of petrol and oil were readily available wherever they were wanted by the armed services and by others such as the fire services and Civil Defence. A particular requirement was the movement of aviation spirit to the many airfields in the eastern counties, and the district manager at Ipswich had three aviation fuel delivery depots under his control, his sector stretching from Southend to Saxmundham and from Ipswich to Haverhill. The photograph, taken in Christchurch Park on 12 October 1945, shows members of the staff based at the Petroleum Board's Eastern Region office in Ipswich.

214/215 Food production was vital to the war effort and every available piece of land was used to grow vegetables. In 1941 Ipswich Corporation Parks Department grew 3,200 early lettuces, 3,000 spring cabbages, 10 cwt. of carrots, 13 cwt. of leeks, 5¼ tons of onions, 5¾ tons of tomatoes and 18½ tons of potatoes, and the following year an additional 57 acres was earmarked to be ploughed up at Chantry and Bourne parks to increase cultivation still further. In addition 125 tons of meadow hay was harvested, and 60 tons of silage was produced. The onion bed above was at Chantry Park. The scene below, which looks as though it might be in the depths of the countryside, is actually just inside the Hadleigh Road entrance to Chantry Park; on top of the load is Herbert Ager, from Gippeswyk Park, and pitching the sheaves to him are Leonard Prior, left, and Mr. K. Goldsmith.

Grow your own . . .

DIG FOR VICTORY

"DIG FOR VICTORY" WEEK

2nd — 7th MARCH, 1942

Programme of Activities

216/217 "Dig for Victory" was the slogan, and in the first week of March 1942 there was a "Dig for Victory" Week that was planned to encourage everyone in the town to produce their own food. There were Ministry of Food films at the Public Hall in Westgate Street, demonstrations of vegetable preservation and exhibitions by allotment holders, the Parks Department, Ipswich School of Arts and Crafts, the East Suffolk County Agricultural Education Committee and other organisations, and at Alexandra Park a model allotment was put on show. Even schoolchildren played their part on the land, like the pupils from Ipswich High School seen in the picture on the right who joined the Ipswich Land Club in 1943.

218 Girls of the Women's Land Army can be seen here operating a Ransomes thrasher and baler on a Suffolk farm.

219 Under the watchful eye of the Ganges figurehead three Wrens prepare for a day out. Left to right, Wrens Gibson, Bitton and Wilkinson, wearing pre August 1942 gabardine hats

220 Pictured outside a sandbagged enclosure are left to right Wrens Orton, Lloyd, Catt and Wilkinson

221 A group of Wrens ready for action in tin hats in 1942! Left to right at the back are Wrens Hughes and Deaves, at the front Wrens Doak, Lane, Rice and Cook

222 A group photograph of Wrens stationed at HMS Ganges in 1942 taken at the base of the mast in front of the Indian Prince figurehead of Ganges

223/224 One of the most famous fighter pilots to serve at Martlesham Heath was Group Captain Douglas Bader, seen here as a wing commander while at the Suffolk station. During his time at Martlesham Heath with No. 242 (F) Squadron in 1940-41 the squadron was flying Hawker Hurricanes, the lower aircraft in the picture above; the other aircraft is the Supermarine Spitfire

225 Later in the war the station was handed over to the United States Army Air Force, which operated three fighter squadrons equipped with the very heavy Republic P.47 Thunderbolts, for which hard runways had to be laid. The control tower seen in the photograph is now home to the Martlesham Heath Aviation Society's museum in which the whole story of this most interesting of aerodromes is told.

226 Although Martlesham Heath continued to be a fighter station after being taken over by the USAAF it did have other visitors from time to time. The aerial view above shows two B.17 Fortresses under repair on the apron, with A and B Flight hangars on the left of the picture. The bombed C Flight hangar can be seen on the right.

227 A Republic P.47 Thunderbolt of the 359th Fighter Squadron that crash-landed on 26 February 1944, killing the pilot, Lieut. William W. Cotter.

228 Two people lost their lives on 8 January 1941 when a stick of ten 50kg. bombs was dropped by a Dornier Do. 17 flying over the Gainsborough Estate on the eastern side of the town. The plane's crew machine-gunned Foxhall Road as it flew off. One of those who died was a woman living in this house in Romney Road which was destroyed by one of the bombs.

229 These houses in Shackleton Road, between Felixstowe Road and Nacton Road, were set on fire by incendiary bombs during a raid on 2 June 1942. Five people, including an ARP warden, were killed in this raid during which incendiary bombs were scattered over a wide area of eastern Ipswich.

230/231 Homes in Bixley Road, seen here from the tower of St. Augustine's Church, were hit during the raid on 2 June 1942, a family of four at no.125 having a remarkable escape when their house was destroyed. They were all in a Morrison shelter, a strong steel cage which could be used as a table when not needed as an indoor shelter; they were among ten people trapped in the rubble of their dwellings, but they emerged more or less unscathed. The Morrison shelter, named after Mr. Herbert Morrison, Home Secretary and Minister of Home Security in Churchill's War Cabinet, can be seen in the middle of the picture below.

232 A woman of 21 was killed in this house in York Road, between Felixstowe Road and Upper Cavendish Street. On the morning after the raid rescue workers are still searching the rubble.

233 Rescue workers had a gruesome task in Lindbergh Road, near the Nacton Road corner, on 25 August 1942 when a bomb scored a direct hit on an Anderson shelter in the garden of one of the houses, killing 14 people. Two houses were destroyed and others damaged. By grim coincidence three people were killed the very next day when an incendiary bomb container struck another Anderson shelter in Avondale Road, off Landseer Road.

234 The Ipswich Corporation Transport depot in Constantine Road was protected by timber revetments and piles of sandbags to cut down the effect of blast from bombs. Other public buildings were also sandbagged as part of the precautions taken early in the war against air raids.

235 Few civilian vehicles were built between 1939 and 1946, almost the entire production of the motor industry going to the forces, but a few vehicles had to be provided to keep businesses going. This Bedford delivery van has no trimmings, but the very simple front bumper is painted white to aid visibility at night; the headlights are masked.

FRASERS
IPSWICH LTD

FRASERS
IPSWICH LTD
TELEPHONE 2191

REMOVALS
STORAGE
CABINETS
CARPETS
CURTAINS

236 As in the earlier war women were brought in to serve the town's public transport undertaking, but this time they served as drivers as well as conductresses. This group photograph of Corporation transport staff was taken just after the war.

237 The all-woman crew of an Ipswich trolleybus during the war, when women were recruited to replace men who had joined the armed services. Both the headlights and the already small sidelights are masked to cut down the amount of light showing during the blackout, but to help make the trolleybus more visible to people on the road the front bumpers are painted white, while there is a white line around the mudguard.

238 An Air Raid Precautions notice adorns the window of this single-deck trolleybus, seen here at the Priory Heath depot in May 1940. The wheel arches and the edges of the steps are painted white to assist passengers trying to board the vehicle during the blackout.

239/240 These houses in Myrtle Road, off Fore Hamlet, were destroyed in an early-morning raid on 2 June 1943 which cost the lives of 11 Ipswich people. In contrast to earlier raids when bombers dropped sticks of bombs from a considerable height, nine Focke-Wulf Fw.190 fighter-bombers roared over at roof-top height, their intended targets no doubt being Ransomes' works and shipping in the Dock. One of the nine aircraft flew into the blast of his companions' bombs, struck the jib of a dockside crane and crashed into the Dock; the pilot died in the crash. Two of those who died in the Myrtle Road bombing were a Mr. and Mrs. Smith, who perished when their house at no.44 was hit by a bomb.

241 Many Suffolk men were captured by the Japanese at the fall of Singapore, and the Lord Lieutenant, the Earl of Stradbroke, organised a special fund to help prisoners of war and their dependents.

242 One of the objectives of the air raids was to disrupt communications, and railway lines were a particular target. On 3 November 1943 a bomb dropped on the line in the Dales area of north Ipswich; this picture of repair work being carried out is taken from the vicinity of Knightsdale Road looking across to Ashcroft Road.

243/244 The firm of Frederick Tibbenham Ltd. in Turret Lane again turned the skills of its employees to the production of aircraft propellers, which were produced in considerable quantity. Above can be seen large four-bladed airscrews at an early stage of manufacture with ten or more laminations being glued together to form the basic shape. Below women are working on the painstaking task of planing the airscrew to shape.

245/246 Propellers for the Airspeed Oxford twin-engined training aircraft undergoing balancing in Tibbenham's works; some have yellow-painted tips designed to make the airscrews visible as the engines were being run up so as to avoid ground crew walking into them. Below are airscrews being loaded on to a large lorry for delivery; compare this with the horse-drawn transport of 20 years earlier shown in picture 82.

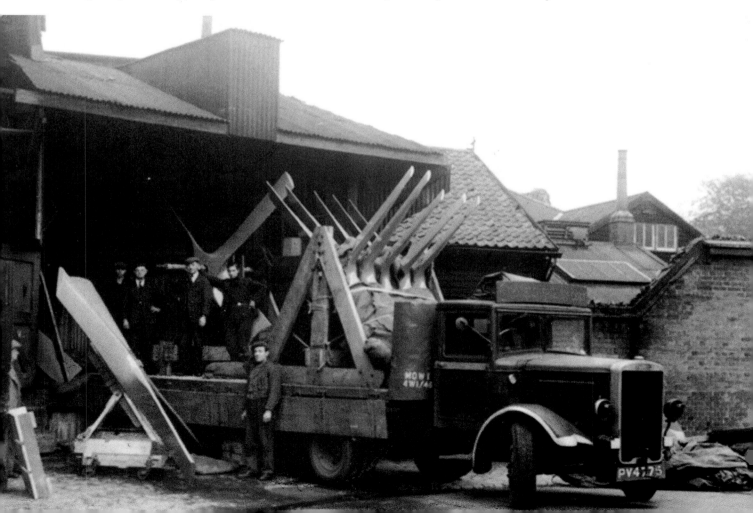

247/249 The "Squander Bug" was an object of derision in wartime Britain and the emphasis was on the need to subscribe to winning the war. In 1942 the target for Ipswich Warship Week was £700,000, and for "Salute the Soldier" Week in 1944 nothing less than a million pounds would do. Ipswich also subscribed to the cost of a Supermarine Spitfire Mk.Vb, seen in the picture above, but as the censor has deleted the serial number and any squadron markings one cannot be entirely certain that it was the one in the photograph.

IPSWICH WARSHIP WEEK
FEBRUARY 28th—MARCH 7th

£700,000
THE TARGET

Save and invest your money with security in any or all of the following Government issues

NATIONAL SAVINGS CERTIFICATES
15/- each, or buy 6d. and 2/6 Stamps
Free of Income Tax

3% DEFENCE BONDS
£5 and multiples of £5

2½% NATIONAL WAR BONDS
1949–1951

3% SAVINGS BONDS
1955-1965

POST OFFICE SAVINGS BANK
and
TRUSTEE SAVINGS BANKS

THE SIGNAL IS SAVE

IPSWICH
"MILLION POUND"
"Salute the Soldier"
WEEK
May 6th to 13th, 1944

BACK YOUR MAN

SAVE ALL YOU CAN

Target—
ONE MILLION POUNDS

2D.

ISSUED BY THE IPSWICH SAVINGS COMMITTEE

250 The Ipswich Museum lecture room was used to house an exhibition of photographs and equipment in order to boost National Savings. The large object in the foreground of the picture is an aerial camera used in reconnaissance aircraft to take photographs of possible targets and to show damage caused by earlier raids.

251/252 Throughout the war years efforts were made to persuade people not to go away for their holidays so as to avoid congestion on the already-busy railways; coastal districts and seaside resorts were in any case largely prohibited areas. Programmes of "holidays-at-home" entertainment were put on throughout the country, and in Ipswich the Royal Marine Band from HMS *Ganges* provided a concert of popular music as part of the programme for 1944; in this 1945 programme the deckchairs brought from Felixstowe helped to provide a holiday atmosphere in Christchurch Park.

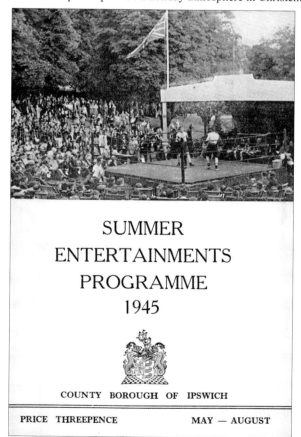

253/254 Towards the end of the war two new weapons were introduced by the Germans, the V1 flying bomb, nicknamed the Doodlebug by the intended victims, and the V2 rocket that climbed into the stratosphere on its way across the North Sea and re-entered at supersonic speed, causing a bang which preceded the explosion of the warhead. The first Doodlebug to fall in the town demolished four houses in Maryon Road on 1 September 1944, and the second destroyed ten houses and killed five people in Halton Crescent on 18 October 1944. Both the pictures are of damage caused by the V1 in Halton Crescent.

255 Another Doodlebug fell on a bungalow close to the 13th-century village church at Chelmondiston in December 1944, virtually destroying the church. It was more than ten years before the church could be rebuilt; post-war circumstances dictated that priority had to be given to other concerns.

256 The last attack on Ipswich, and possibly the last air raid on Britain, came on 4 March 1945, when bombs dropped in Seymour Road, Over Stoke. Nine people were killed and six houses were destroyed in this last raid. Altogether 225 houses in Ipswich had been destroyed by enemy action and another 774 had been severely damaged.

257/258 With Allied forces advancing into Germany in April and May 1945 everyone was seized with a feeling of relief; the end could not be far off. As news spread of the German capitulation crowds gathered in Tower Ramparts, above, but there was no sign of the ostentatious jubilation that is seen in pictures of celebrations in London. There would be time for that when Japan, too, was defeated and the many Suffolk men held in Japanese prison camps were on their way home. And nobody expected the war in the Pacific to be over in less than three months. When news came at last of the surrender document being signed on Luneburg Heath the families' rations were somehow stretched to provide food for the children at street parties, like that below in Waterworks Street, that celebrated Victory in Europe.

259 Residents of Edgar Street, Portman Street, Priory Street and James Street all got together in James Street to celebrate VE Day. These little streets in which so many people once lived have all disappeared under the Greyfriars development.

260 "Found at last, cremation tonight" reads the placard on the Hitler effigy that loomed over the street party in Brunswick Road, off Woodbridge Road. Bonfires had been banned during the war, and Guy Fawkes had escaped his annual roasting; now the people of Ipswich had a new Guy to burn.

261/262 In Long Street some of the children donned home-made paper hats for the VE Day party, but in the grounds of St. John's Church in Cauldwell Hall Road, below, there seemed a certain lack of gaiety about the children; perhaps their dads were still away, fighting the Japanese in the Pacific.

263/264 In Gatacre Road a large propeller, possibly one of those manufactured by Tibbenhams in Turret Lane, served as a table decoration at the VE street party, and in Grange Road, below, an American serviceman, centre back, joined in the celebrations.

265/266 Almost every street in Ipswich celebrated with some kind of a street party. Above the residents of Shakespeare Road, a part of Whitton developed only just before the war, gather to mark the coming of peace, but only two or three lucky soldiers have managed to obtain leave; apart from them only women and children are there. There are more men at the tea party in Sidegate Lane, but they are all beyond the first flush of youth.

267 A garden in Phoenix Road, between Woodbridge Road and Rushmere Road, was the setting for this VE party at which a great effort had been put into the decorations.

268 The children of Wallace Road, between Bramford Road and Bramford Lane, turn out in force to celebrate Victory in Europe, but there is still a sombre look on many of the faces. It isn't over yet, they seem to say.

269/270 Do the strains of wartime life show on the faces of some of these people gathered outside the Golf Hotel in Foxhall Road? At Westerfield, below, villagers gathered in a meadow opposite the old post office to celebrate the coming of peace in Europe.

271/272 The few adult males in this group seem to be trying to give themselves extra prominence by standing high at the back. There is just one man in uniform to be seen in this group in Brookfield Road, that odd loop off Springfield Lane; most men were away, some preparing for the hoped-for invasion of Japan. The youngsters below, including one in his pram who wonders what it's all about, are celebrating outside the Margaret Catchpole Hotel in Cliff Lane.

273/274 When Japan capitulated after the dropping of atomic bombs on the cities of Hiroshima and Nagasaki there was another round of parties for the children of Ipswich. At last there was a real hope that the menfolk who were in the services would soon be home, and there was also the hope that the survivors of the notorious Japanese prison camps might be on their way home. The VJ tea above was held in Spring Road, and the fancy dress party below was held in Fletcher Road on the Gainsborough Estate on 7 September 1945.

275 Many men had been conscripted into the services before they had had time to establish a career, and one of the first priorities was to train men for civilian work. These are catering staff at a training centre set up at Ipswich Airport just after the war; Daphne Preston, who provided the photograph, is on the left of the group.

276 Quite a lot of the demobilised men joined the British Legion in a bid to preserve the comradeship that had been perhaps the single redeeming feature of wartime service life. The Ipswich branch of the British Legion had its own band, which was much in demand for Remembrance Day parades and other events.

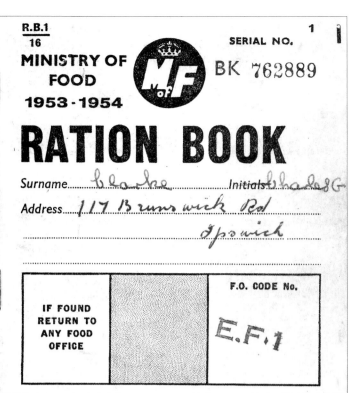

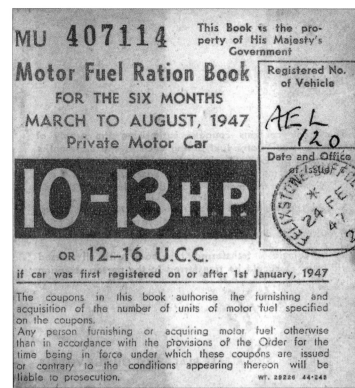

277/277A The effects of war were felt for many years after it finished, with rationing of meat, eggs, fat, cheese, bacon, sugar, tea, sweets, clothing and petrol continuing into the 1950s.

278 Queues were a normal feature of wartime life, particularly when there was something special to be had. What were people queuing for at Herbert Wells, the pork butchers opposite Fore Street baths, one wonders?

279/280 The Freedom of Entry to the Borough was granted to the Suffolk Regiment on 5 June 1948 in Christchurch Park. Afterwards, led by the regimental band and a colour party, detachments of the 4th Battalion, the 1st Cadet Battalion and the Old Comrades' Association marched through the town, exercising their newly-given right of marching through the Borough with drums beating, bands playing, colours flying and bayonets fixed. In the pictures the parade is passing the saluting base on the Cornhill. The Suffolk Regiment, the 12th Foot, later amalgamated with the Royal Norfolk Regiment as the 1st Battalion The Royal Anglian Regiment.

281/282 Two memorials stand side by side on the Barrack Square at Martlesham Heath, one to RAF men and the other to men of the USAAF who died while flying from the airfield. These photographs show the unveiling of the American memorial, which was dedicated in 1946 and was the first such memorial to members of the USAAF to be erected after the Second World War. The memorial to men of the Royal Flying Corps, the Royal Air Force and Dominion and Commonwealth forces and to civilian personnel who lost their lives while serving at the station was dedicated much more recently, in 1991.

283 In the 1950s Martlesham Heath was home to the Spitfire and Hurricane of the Battle of Britain Flight, which was based in B Flight hangar. It was from Martlesham that the annual Battle of Britain flypast was made over London, but the Flight moved to Coltishall in Norfolk about 1960.

284 The last aircraft to be tested at Martlesham Heath was a civilian airliner, the Avro 748 G-ARAY, which was employed in rough ground trials in 1963. Part of the airfield was broken up to provide loose, sandy ground for the trials, which resulted in the Avro 748 being chosen as the basis of a new short takeoff and landing transport aircraft for the RAF. The new plane eventually entered service in 1966 as the Hawker Siddeley Andover.

285 On Friday 21 July 1961 HM Queen Elizabeth inspects the Royal Guard and Queen's Colour of the Portsmouth Command at HMS Ganges.

286 Boys from HMS Ganges march through the town centre after receiving the Freedom of the County Borough of Ipswich in 1971.

287 The last ceremonial Mast Manning at Ganges was on Parents' Day on 6th June 1973. In this photograph the height the boys climbed is clearly seen. The boy on the top was known as the button boy. Although there were safety nets it must have taken considerable courage to climb the mast, particularly for the first time. Accidents did happen, including fatalities. In 1918 so many boys climbed the mast to celebrate the end of the Great War that the stanchions holding the safety net gave way, causing several injuries. In 1949 one boy fell head first from the mast, and his head went straight through the net, stripping all the skin off his neck.

288 above: Flying came to an end at Martlesham Heath in 1979, a number of light aircraft being flown in for the official last day of flying on 25 March of that year. Already the remaining section of runway was overshadowed by the Suffolk Police headquarters, and more of the old airfield was soon to be occupied by the new village developed in the 1980s. The nearest aircraft is a de Havilland Hornet Moth which had first flown at Martlesham Heath in 1937; local aeronautical author Gordon Kinsey is being interviewed by the BBC beside the aircraft.

289 A public house was opened in 1979 as part of the new village developed on the former airfield and named The Douglas Bader. To mark the opening the Battle of Britain Memorial Flight made a ceremonial flypast; leading the flight is a de Havilland Devon, with the Hawker Hurricane to starboard and the Supermarine Spitfire to port. The buildings of the Post Office Research Station, now the BT Research Station, form the background to the picture.

290/291 In 1992 the Royal Army Medical Corps was granted the Freedom of Entry in recognition of the long association of the corps with Ipswich; the 1st East Anglian Field Ambulance, a Territorial Army unit, was based at the Woodbridge Road drill hall for many years. The photograph above shows the band of the RAMC marching across Cornhill on 18 February 1992, after the formal granting of the honour, and in the picture below the Mayor, Mrs. Joan Cubbin, is seen speaking to Mr. Harold Ellis, M.M., a former member of the 1st East Anglian Field Ambulance. Left to right are Lieut.-Col. John Hamilton, Mr. Ellis, Lieut.-Col. Sue Payne, Mrs. Cubbin, General Sir Peter Beal, Director General of Army Medical Services, and Colonel Richard Croese.

292 A Sherman tank in the grounds of Orwell Park School pictured with boys from the school, their Head, Andrew Auster, and the Rev John Waller and the Rev John Fisher. This photograph was taken in September 2001 at a reunion of survivors of the 1st Royal Tank Regiment of the 7th Armoured Division, the 'Desert Rats', who were based at the school in 1944 while preparing for the D-Day landings.

293 In March 2002 the Freedom of the Borough of Ipswich was granted to the Wattisham-based 4 Regiment Army Air Corps. In the picture troops from the regiment present arms on the Cornhill during the presentation ceremony, which included an inspection by Ipswich Mayor Maureen Carrington-Brown.

294 HMS Grafton, seen here passing under the Orwell bridge, is a type 23 frigate affiliated to the town of Ipswich. She is the eighth Royal Navy vessel to bear the name and was commissioned in May 1997. Since her affiliation with Ipswich further links have been developed with local businesses, 4 Regiment Army Air Corps and the TS Orwell Sea Cadet unit. Her commanding officer is Commander Richard Thomas, MBE.